Lil Southern Belle

Kalena Amos

TABLE OF CONTENTS

INTRODUCTION — A NAME AIN'T A HALO...

They tell me we're family, as if blood is supposed to be a blindfold. As if sharing a last name excuses turning your head away from abuse, from pimping, from molestation, from the quiet erasure of innocence wrapped in forced silence and church hymns. You listened to the streets more than you ever listened to your own children and grandchildren, then demanded loyalty like it was owed instead of earned. That alone is disturbing.

You poisoned my name with a precision so cruel it felt ritualistic... like the rarest kind of voodoo... then stood in church with your hands raised, begging God to answer your cries. He's probably tired of hearing. Faith without accountability is just performance, and hell looks overcrowded with people who pray loud and live rotten. I don't regret you. I regret allowing you a role in my timeline at all.

Everyone who harmed me, who spoke about my child, who robbed me of innocence before I knew it was something worth protecting—those roots run straight through my mother's bloodline. And somewhere deep down, she knows it. The kind of knowing that cries in the quiet, the kind that doesn't absolve but only echoes. I've been paying for sins that were never mine, carrying consequences passed down like cursed heirlooms, while the guilty perfected the art of denial.

No accountability, yet always claiming representation...family, mother, elder...as if titles could replace truth. That's not tradition; that's insanity rehearsed until it feels normal. I refuse to turn the other cheek; one of them already let harm feel at home there. Funny how life circles back on itself...cheap, hollow, plastic promises dressed up as hope...always exposed, always repeating.

So find another alibi. Rewrite the story if you need to. But don't expect me to play confused while the truth is this loud. I see it all now. And that's the part you'll never forgive me for.

CHAPTER 1 — SOUTHERN SOIL

The road I came upon was red dirt and silence. The kind of silence that teaches you early how to listen for danger. Folks say the South has sweet tea and manners, but it also got doors that close quiet and hands that swing loud. I learned both before I learned long division.

Imagine being me...small enough that bruises could be explained away as clumsiness and big enough to know lies when they're ironed flat and pressed into church clothes. Every mark had a story ready for the company. Every question from school came with a warning look at home. We didn't air dirty laundry; we burned it in the backyard and told the smoke to keep its mouth shut.

I lost my mama the way people lose things in this world...not all at once, but piece by piece. First, her voice got tired. Then her eyes learned how to look past me. Then one morning, she was just... gone. And the house didn't mourn. It adjusted. Like losing a limb and learning how to walk anyway.

They spoke about me like I was a backdoor prayer...said quick, never meant to be answered. I was hidden when the company came, tucked away like a shame that might ask questions. Schools asked about my body like it was a chalkboard full of answers nobody wanted to read. Family told me to be quiet so the picture stayed pretty. Smile so the lie held.

I learned how to take a hit and how to disappear in the same breath. Learned how to apologize for bleeding. Learned how to keep defending myself against people who taught me how to be defenseless. Family was smoke and mirrors...always shifting, always making you doubt what you just saw. If I spoke up, I was ungrateful. If I stayed quiet, I was loyal. Either way, I paid.

There were days I stood so close to God I could feel the heat of Him. Days when living felt like a dare I kept losing. But something stubborn lived in my chest... a mean, quiet hope. It told me to get up even when I wanted the ground to finish me off. Told me to keep walking even when the road felt like punishment.

The whole mama's side hated me for being a reflection. Mirrors make liars nervous. I looked at what they didn't fix. I sounded like what they buried. So they talked. Lord, they talked. Years of it. Gossip sat high and comfortable while real work went undone. Patterns stayed broken because fixing them would cost pride.

I survived just to get tired of surviving. I waited on death like a golden ticket some nights and thought about how rest must feel when you don't have to claim anybody anymore. But then there was my sister... lost and found and lost again to the needle... And I swallowed my pride and prayed she'd live one more sunrise. Love will keep you here even when you're ready to go.

Once, in public, someone threw gasoline on me like a joke. Laughter burned hotter than the sting. I didn't catch fire that day, but I learned something: people will strike a match if they think you won't flame back.

So I kept walking. Cold steps. Southern dust. Spine straight, heart scarred. I didn't come out soft. I came out honest. And if you ask me now... Could you walk a mile in my shoes? I don't need an answer. I already did. And I'm still here & still living through it ....

CHAPTER 2 – BLOOD AIN'T ALWAYS COVER

Continuing on... I was raised where the heat makes folks reckless, and the truth gets slow-cooked into lies. Down South, we call it tradition when it's really just survival dressed up in Sunday shoes.

Imagine being me...grown early, priced like livestock, the minds around me stuck in the old days where a girl's body was currency and silence was respect. They talked about me like a raggedy mule but still checked my teeth, my hips, and my worth. Highest bidder mentality with family faces. The same mouths that said blood is thicker stayed counting what I could bring in, not who I was.

I was only visible when I was bragging rights. Look what we got. Look what she can do. Look what she brings. But when shame walked into the room, I got hid like a secret nobody wanted to talk about. I was income feeding the ungrateful and bastardized, a paycheck with a pulse. Love never clocked in, but expectation stayed on overtime.

Imagine growing up in a house that felt like a whorehouse... doors never really closed, boundaries never taught, and sex floating in the air like cigarette smoke. You breathe it in before you even know what it is. Then one day, they point at you and call you a hoe, like exposure wasn't forced on you and like innocence didn't get stolen right out of your hands and blamed on your grip.

Life is so crazy it feel like it should be illegal. Delusion dances real close to mental illness in folks who forget the role they played, rewrite the script, and then swear they are saints. Trauma don't get replaced. It sits. It waits. But I learned I could heal and still tell the truth without asking permission.

Men hated me for what they took from me. Disgusted by the mirror I held up just by existing. Cursed me to produce again... another body, another dollar, another sacrifice... while saying we family, like that made it holy. Funny how family always got a handout and a blindfold on.

If these walls could talk, I'd be rich. They seen everything... every deal, every lie, every night nobody came to defend me proper. But down here, folks say every family just sweeps dirt into the road and lets somebody else run it over.

So here I stand... reckless with my truth, Southern to the bone, tired of swallowing history that never belonged to me. The question ain't whether I can keep fighting.

It's about whether the world is ready for what happens when I don't shut up anymore....

CHAPTER 3 — WATCHFUL GIRLS

Down here, my life started on the back porch of things folks don't talk about. Heat hanging heavy, flies knowing more secrets than people do. Imagine being me... only allowed to bathe in a dog pan, the water gone cold before the dirt ever came off. They fed us spoiled leftovers in the house... us, as my sister and I... Even though government food was on the shelves, somehow I was still digging through dumpsters for little prizes, half-broken joys, and anything that felt like a reward. And still, I guarded my little sister like a last hymn, even while respect was getting beat and spent wrong... passed around like tithe money that never reached God.

Truth got a way of circling back in the South. It don't knock. It just shows up. Imagine being me, never having what was gifted...only what was thrifted, patched together with shame and prayer...because the church demanded their dues while running up personal bills on my back. Praise on Sunday, cruelty on Monday. Chaos everywhere you looked, like it was part of the décor.

I was a high-paid slave dressed up in responsibility. Paid well enough to keep quiet, but never enough to be free. Heads tilted down at me, eyes saying what mouths wouldn't: you were never meant to marry in, just to work in. But I was supposed to be cool. Smile. Swallow it. "Everybody makes mistakes," they say... just not like mine. Mine depended on the weather, the liquor, and the mood of the room.

I got yelled at, stepped on, and treated like trash just so I could be turned into a joke later. Years down the line, I learned the truth: the one I trusted most hated me, all because of a lie they let live too long. Funny how people turn white as ghosts when the truth walks back in the house like it owns the place.

Ain't enough soap in this world to wash the blood off your hands... not the kind you spill inside somebody. The way you wrecked my sister and me left cries stuck in the walls. Echoes so loud even the spirits wander restless through the halls. At night, you can hear them... floors creaking with memory, air heavy with what never got fixed. But we family, right?

They found wicked delight in pretending nothing happened. Beer bottles clinking, alcohol swallowing every real conversation. That was the least of the fights. You were "stable," they said... yet fried, preserved in your own poison like embalming fluid. Corrupted like jail doors slamming shut, over and over. Still, we family, right?

And then there was Mother Dearest... a dog carrying the bone, passing lies mouth to mouth. When I needed help, I got smacked and tossed aside. Now it's silence. Folks wandering through town acting confused, like they don't know how it all went wrong.

Imagine my pain being everyone else's pleasure. Imagine realizing the truth that you survived is going to be their greatest regret. That part? I'll treasure it. Because down South, reckoning comes slow... but when it arrives, it stays.

CHAPTER 4 — PROJECT LESSONS

The South got a way of smiling while it's hurting you.

Imagine being me... years rolling by like cicadas screaming the same lie every summer. By the time I hit school, folks weren't looking at my face; they were counting my bruises. Teachers whispering. Phones clicking shut. Family suddenly close enough to touch but too distant to save you. Blood don't mean brave down here—it means quiet.

Then, one morning, everything shifted. FBI cars in my grandmother's yard, red dirt kicked up like the land itself was testifying. Neighbors watching from porches, like it was entertainment. I got moved to an aunt's house, told to pack light and speak lighter. Did I survive? Of course. Southern kids survive by learning how to lie clean and early... especially when you're protecting the very ones breaking you. You tell yourself they care. You tell yourself love just hurts like this.

After the investigation, it was right back where I started. Same heat. Same rules. Same "stay in a child's place." Hands in the garden dirt while grown folks laughed on the porch. A fresh deck of cards slapped down, spades cracking like gunshots, drinks sweating in glass jars. That's when the games would start... and I don't mean cards.

Imagine being hated by uncles who only listened when they were in a frenzy... high as the sky and low in their spirits. Depressed the same way the women they passed through were depressed, used up, and left empty like a test run gone wrong. They came and went, and the house stayed a horror show. I couldn't tell you how many glasses shattered or how many guns were pointed too close to my face and my sister's. Laughter followed the violence sometimes...laughing at scars, at blood running where it shouldn't. I was filled with rage, the kind that sits heavy in the chest, and nobody cared.

Evil don't announce itself down here. It wanders. It checks rooms. It waits until no adult is looking. And when you don't know what normal feels like, you learn to disappear. You hide first. Then you harden. That's when the anger comes...not loud, not wild...just steady. You rebel because something crossed a door that was never supposed to be opened.

But Grandma couldn't see it—or wouldn't. She was too wrapped up in dollar bills and a rotted piece of a man, the kind the South keeps alive out of habit. Everything justified. Everything excused. Watching how easily men moved through life was enough to teach me resentment without a lesson plan.

The truth didn't matter until their business started leaking out. That's when concern showed up dressed like panic.

There was only one place I ever felt safe. My Aunt Jerry. Proud Southern sweet tea, soft laughter, and a heart that didn't ask questions just to judge the answers. She never looked at me like I was broken. She helped me. Held space for my sister and me together, like she knew we'd be stronger that way. When she threw parties and I could escape my own personal hell, I felt something close to love. For a moment, that was enough.

But jealousy always finds a way into houses full of snakes. Someone always has to be the host for poison. I never understood why God made me for them... why I was placed in a family that taught me solitude before safety. They were the reason I learned to walk alone, to choose my own current, and to swim even when the water was cold and unforgiving.

When Child Protective Services finally came, hell didn't break loose. Hell had been loose. They just finally smelled it. The truth was written in the stains on my clothes, in my body, in the sweat-and-shame stench nobody wanted to name.

Southern grandmas say, "We family."

But family don't always mean protection.

Sometimes it just means silence.

And kids?

Kids are always "too young" to fight—

until they grow up cold enough to tell it themselves.

CHAPTER 5 — CHURCH WITHOUT HEALING

They say the South got a way of naming you before you even know your own name.

They said I was a preteen, but rumors moved faster than age ever could. Glide after glide, whispers sliding across porches and kitchen tables—talking about me like I was grown, like I was something dirty they could pass around with a laugh. "Hot in the ass," they said. Friends of the family, homeboys in ruined houses, men who never knew a single piece of me but swore they did. Jealousy sat deep in it, buried under fake concern and loud mouths.

And me? I was just a kid, minding my own business, not even knowing what life was yet. All I really knew was the sound of cards slapping a table and grown folks yelling over nothing. My only real worry was my baby sister. That was it: Protect her. Stay close. That's how we survived.

But even that got twisted.

They called us incestual lesbians—words we didn't even understand yet. Imagine that: two little girls trying to shield each other from a seasonal kind of crazy, sharing blood and fear, and somehow that turns into something perverse in grown minds. How you even come up with that? The sickness wasn't in us... It was watching us too closely.

I watched my grandmother church-hop like it washed her clean, switching men the same way she switched dishes. Scrubbed on the surface but still dirty underneath. My two uncles stayed clung to her like dogs chasing a scent—washed up, restless, and always hovering. Everybody talked. Bullshit walked freely. In that house, it felt normal—or at least that's what I was taught to believe.

It didn't hit me right away how broken a family could be. Not until Child Protective Services showed up. Not gently—snatching me like I was evidence that needed to be removed. The looks on their faces weren't stitched with care; they were angry, panicked, and exposed. Calls scattered like roaches on cornbread—too many voices. Too much scrambling. Funny how nobody looks ahead until the door gets kicked in.

Guilt and anger bounced through distant phone calls, everybody trying to figure out how they were gonna get out of it. Not how to fix it … but how to escape it.

I left with my heart hollowed out. Separated from my sister. Left her standing in insanity while I was carried off with nothing but fear and silence. That's when I learned how to pray... not because I was holy, but because I needed something small and steady to guide me when everything else felt like a stray bullet.

Uncles. Cousins. Family friends. Nobody knowing where to start telling the truth. Life felt like a joke dressed up as tradition. But still, we family, right?

Questions should've been asked. But how could they be when the devil stood right there with a glow-in-the-dark halo? Her offspring lined up to defend her, because trauma don't disappear... It just passes hands. What came before me had already torn everything up.

The crazy thing is, here we are.

Calling it family don't make it safe.

And kids shouldn't have to carry the battle wounds of other people's sins, sorrows, and scars.

That's the cold truth the South don't like to say out loud.

CHAPTER 6 — SILENCE AS INHERITANCE

They always say that the South loves to say "time heals," but somehow the bullshit just disappears instead.

All it ever gave me was how could you and she be lying again... lies stacked on lies, dressed up clean enough to pass for truth. Family don't mean much when blood washes off that easy. It's just another coping mechanism, but nobody ever asked the right questions. They just decided.

I was young. Scared. Barely a teen. Still dirty...not from sin, but from neglect. Nobody taught me how to wash myself. Cleanliness wasn't a thing when your life sat in the hands of a hoarder. You get used to filth when filth is all that's offered. Then they said I was "free."

Somewhat.

Not quite.

I told my story, and it came right back at me—flipped, twisted, and swinging like the beatings I used to get on the regular. But we family, right? Deflection became a sport. Even the top dogs ignored the cries because they never cared. Most of them were coached anyway—rehearsed like suspects being searched for something forbidden. Blood thicker than water? Yeah—thick with unhealed sins that keep answering roll call.

"Stay in a child's place."

"Grown folks talking."

I heard that everywhere—even in stranger places full of even more broken kids. That's when I started questioning myself. I got placed with someone who smelled like old sweat and bad choices. A house full of kids and dirty stripper money. No preparation. No softness. "Food-stamp junkie" is what I wanted to call my first foster mom. Way out in the boondocks. Trailer air mixed with sour mop water. The kids were rough but cool...like a midnight breeze. Comfort showed up. Freedom didn't.

Calls kept coming. Family still yelling, Leave her in the system. All she do is lie. Meanwhile, the whorehouse of voodoo stayed open, prayer in one hand, poison in the other, still pulling in the innocent. Do you ever learn—or is it just heads buried too deep to see daylight?

I was still a kid.

And we family, right?

The eldest son knew the game. Stayed in his lane. His wife...nose tilted high, proper as porcelain...never wanted to touch what we were. She did kind things sometimes, sure. Time passed. Death passed. Still didn't change her distance. Hurt like that don't dissolve. But we family, right?

I watched Southern women stitch broken men back together piece by piece—proud of the hoe, loyal to the bottle's stink, choosing him over blood. Crazy. Normal. That's why I learned to fight. Sex was power and weakness all wrapped up; might as well call it voodoo for the things it makes people justify.

I still had hope, though. Mind. Body. Spirit.

But turning fourteen into fifteen will knock the wind out of you. Suicidal thoughts rolled in like bass from a trunk... Do it, do it. My heart said no, even when my head begged for quiet. I stayed.

Then the second placement came. Mrs. Ammons...sweet as a balm, beautiful enough to stop men mid-sentence. I still didn't fit. Groomed. Broken. Labeled. Eventually, I lost it and landed in a mental facility.

But we family, right?

Look what you did.

That's when it finally settled in, cold and permanent:

Family ain't blood.

Family ain't church.

Family ain't who hurts you and calls it love.

Family really ain't shit—

And surviving them was the first real thing I ever did.

CHAPTER 7 — POP POP DOUGLAS

They say time heals things. Folks love to say that down here, usually right after Sunday service, right before they go back to minding everybody else's business. You'd think after all that time I spent locked behind the white walls in a mental ward, the scars would've closed up neat and clean. But no. Same wounds, just dressed up different. Same church-bedding wench hovering close, gathering scraps of whatever slipped out my mouth like gossip was communion wine.

I got sent right back to the place my spirit already knew it didn't belong. That's when I first heard about a group home in Boaz, Alabama... Right around the same time my caseworker, Mrs. Kilgroe, quit. I can still see her face: red, snotty, tears falling fast and hot, like she finally understood the mess she was leaving me in. She knew. Lord, she knew.

I stayed there crying through months that felt longer than summers, not knowing which way was north or if it even mattered. Then word came about some distant cousins up in a city with clean sidewalks and quiet nights. Upper-class folks. Folks who didn't yell just to hear their own echoes. And somehow, they became the blessing I never knew to pray for. With them, confidence crept back into my bones. They didn't save me... But they showed me I wasn't unsavable.

My little respected trio, plus a few, guided me in different ways. Showed me that better existed. And for that, I gave praise. Still, I never quite fit. Evil got greedy. It always does.

At seventeen, I said yes to moving in with a man I wish had stayed gone. The one who abandoned my mama, remarried, and called himself my father. Up north, blood; down south, damage. Folks called him a leech, a scam, a scab that never healed right.

He had his own rugrats and his own mess and still found room to ruin me. He didn't earn my presence, didn't credit the hands that raised me, didn't respect the roots that kept me sane.

Why imagine a perfect family when it's stitched together with corruption and sin?

That move tore me clean out of the ground. Everything rotted again. Maybe God was testing me—seeing if I'd still trust Him when the lesson hurt. I did. I do. But that trust cost me dearly.

To him, I was paperwork. Easy money. A quick check to flash and forget. The calls never stopped... Where she at? What she saying? As if I wasn't fighting just to keep my mind steady. He came at me sideways with things he "heard," like he was part of the crew, like he knew me at all. Just another man craving women like a fix, like love was something to consume instead of give.

All I wanted was a hug.

But "We family, right?"

Selfish as hell. No accountability. Just use, discard, repeat. Karma circled but never landed where it should. He dished people out like medicine he refused to take himself. Never changed. Not once. Not for a day.

The woman he dated wasn't much to look at, but her spirit screamed louder than the bruises I saw on her. Fear sat heavy in my chest. What do you do when telling the truth costs you peace? You bite your lip. You shut the hell up. You obey.

But "we family, right?"

Everybody knew. Everybody carried on. Same folks wondering later why I looked hollow, why my eyes stayed tired. I got sick of being a puppet. Sick of strings I never agreed to. So I said fuck it and walked back into the system.

Again.

Not this again.

Same walls. Same questions. Same woman asking what I'd been saying, when the truth was I was unraveling, and it didn't even matter anymore. Because when nobody listens, your silence becomes the loudest thing you own.

And down here in the South, silence can kill you just as easy as truth.

CHAPTER 8 — FALSE AUTHORITY

Imagine my surprise... years and years flew by
still trapped in the system,
watched by hungry eyes that never meant to save me,
only count me.
I survived off motion:
dancing, working, changing states, changing names,
learning how to disappear without dying.
My foster mama, Bervie,
Memphis-made, bad to the bone.
No sugar in her voice, no shame in her eyes.
Every word she spoke came with weight behind it.
We loved each other sideways...
rough, necessary, never soft.
But when I needed her,
she showed up.
That mattered.
I became a woman under ceilings raining cash,
grease-stained floors,
customers barking orders like hunger was a language.
Life didn't slow down to let me catch my breath.
It never does.

Big Daddy Mike looked at me like ownership,
like something bright he could flash in the dark.
"A diamond," he thought.
I did what I had to do
to keep the lights on.
Bills paid, dignity thinning.
Then something in me snapped—
clean, final.
Nothing left to explain.
Courtesy and Anna...
Savannah soil in their blood.
Good chicks, sharp minds,
skin kissed by different suns.
Chocolate and brown paid their way
through rooms that never loved us.
We learned fast.
Then came the calls.
New caseworkers.
Same voices, different names.
A domestic fight cracked the house open
and freedom came dressed as eviction.
Eighteen years old.
No landing place.
Just "go."
So I ran back home...

back to the clowns,
the loudmouths,
the lies that never aged.
What I thought I escaped
had roots deep in Southern dirt.
My grandmother stood proud,
just like always.
Pride hides rot well.
Here came the looks,
the whispers,
calling me a thief
like that could erase what she did.
Jealous of my face,
my youth,
my survival.
As if beauty ever saved me.
She sold herself on price tags and men,
hid abortions like sins under church clothes,
praised a pastor while birthing secrets,
raised money but not children.
And still, jealousy burned.
Her son—
trench water mean.
His fists landed like gunshots.
She watched.

She laughed.
Let him step on my neck
and called it family.
So tell me…
how do you respect people
who see you as income,
not blood?
They preach "forgiveness,"
Say "forget."
say family like it's holy.
I believed them once.
That was the lie.
Cold don't come from winter.
It comes from learning
who never meant to love you and still willing to survive.

CHAPTER 9 — LOVE THAT HOLDS HOSTAGE

Here we go again...

I was eighteen when I came back to Anniston, Alabama

thinking time might've cooled what fire couldn't burn down.

Shelby dropped me off and drove away

and the weight hit my chest before my feet hit the ground.

Same streets. Same sins.

Different year.

Same ending waiting.

There stood my uncle—

eyes cooked in drugs, a mouth full of nothing.

And my granny,

church-hopping, Bible-clutching,

wearing God like perfume to cover the rot.

I thought, "Lord, what's next?"

I already knew the answer.

I tried to work.

I tried to mind my business.

But my grandma worked harder—

playing telephone to the church,

spreading my name like gossip was communion.

They barely cared about her
until their pews started emptying,
and suddenly my life was useful again.
They think they know me.
All they ever saw was a smile stitched with blood.
I was forced into church just to be discussed,
picked apart,
judged by people who never asked what broke me.
Victory Headquarters—that was the name.
That was the last Sunday they ever saw me.
If they knew the woman they adored
was the main villain in the story she told,
they might've shut their mouths.
But lies sound holy when you dress them right.
Her son…
a terrorist in a grown man's body—
always talking loud,
like he didn't pimp women just to have a couch to sleep on.
His lies were thick as chicken grease,
slick enough to slide him through life
without ever cleaning the damage he left behind.
I tried to isolate again.
Thought maybe silence would save me.
But my grandma don't let peace live long.
She made sure I was thrown out—again.

This time I didn't beg.
I swallowed my pride and learned fast.
The eldest had a daughter—
questionable, grateful on the surface,
rotten behind closed doors.
Snorting, swinging fists at the woman who birthed her.
But we family, right?
Another state.
Another house.
Months of breathing just enough to heal.
I got what I needed...
and felt the shift.
Not loved.
Just tolerated.
Watched like a suspect.
Monitored like I was locked up.
That told me everything.
So I left.
At nineteen, I collected what was owed to me
and planned my exit, quiet and clean.
Recycled prayers.
Moved smart.
Stayed around people who broke me
long enough to survive.
But don't confuse blood with bond.

Some of y'all ain't family.
You just sick.
Church-going, loud-mouthed,
slick with scripture,
but not enough dirt in this whole Southern ground
to cover the blood, you keep pretending it ain't there.
And that's the coldest truth I know.

CHAPTER 10 — PAIN HAD A VOICE

Imagine being me at nineteen—

monitored like a parolee by married folks with last names and secrets,

family back-paging family,

asking, "What she saying? What she doing?"

Like my existence was a crime scene that never closed.

Imagine being set up to witness blood betray blood...

watching her own flesh snort lines

in the comfort of her husband's other house.

And I had to sit there,

quiet,

listening to how we are trash,

how we are disposable.

But we family, right?

No amount of money could buy my loyalty

to a woman who worships her degrees like trophies,

parades her daughters like proof of success

even when they cracked under silver spoons.

They talk upbringing,

but it was paper-plastic dressed in cubic zirconia.

Loud shine.

No weight.

How we family
But nobody admits they're fools?
I remember the calls.
The voicemails.
My grandma running surveillance like a warden,
calling her siblings:
Check on her. What she saying? She rebellious.
Rebellious—
that's what truth sounds like to liars.
They bury testimonies in the dentures of the Bible,
smiling scripture with rotten gums.
You call yourself daughter, mother, church, accomplished—
a pick-me sellout of a people you step on.
So tell me—
why was I born into a mental institution
disguised as family?
Days passed.
Drama don't sleep.
Her daughter—Barbie-faced and hollow—
wanted smoke with a brat half her age.
Pillow talking old wounds back to life,
then puffing her chest like I owed her fear.
I never gave her a reason.
I was still a kid.
Learning adulthood

from an aunt who listened but never protected.
Crazy, right?
I was in love.
Focused.
Trying not to drown in the extra bullshit.
But here come the watchers again.
A cousin assigned like a camera. What she saying now?
Can I just exist?
I had nobody.
My business ran through mouths
of relatives I never met,
connected by blood but allergic to truth.
But we family, right?
My uncle stood there
while his woman stayed front and center—
cock-eyed,
hyena laughing at other people's pain.
And I'm supposed to respect that?
Then they wanted somebody to beat my ass.
a weak move from people
who almost died twice
and still learned nothing.
Couldn't be me.
Everyone dressed like a millionaires,
posing in pressed lies,

while blood crept up on the tumbleweeds behind them.

Southern soil knows the truth.

It always does.

So imagine being me...

nineteen,

alone,

still standing in it.

And tell me again

How we family when your vultures in disguise...

Waiting for ya next meal or come up with ya hand up and ya ass out.

CHAPTER 11 — WATCHING AND LEARNING

Continuing on...

I was nineteen, still breathing the same air I wasn't wanted in.

Tolerated like a stray dog on a screened-in porch.

A glass of lemonade sweating in my hand, sweet and sour like the lie of "you can stay"—

when really, I was never supposed to be there at all.

Why agree to shelter me just to grind your disgust into my skin?

Every breath I took felt invoiced.

Every mistake I made—small, human, harmless—was treated like I'd reached for luxury.

"Can't afford that," you'd say.

Afford what?

Blood-stained dollars? Pride buried in cow shit?

You were sharp in the head, a coward in the chest—

married into my bloodline just to resent it from the first heartbeat.

Secrets lived on your floors like dust.

I stepped over them daily, barefoot, learning where not to look.

I planned my escape quiet—that was my only indulgence.

You had a daughter raised feral and forgiven.

Yet cursed mine like guilt was hereditary.
You threw hands the same way the past did—
left swelling, left silence.
But we were family, right?
So I swallowed it.
I left with eleven hundred dollars and no goodbye.
Called a taxi like a prayer; I didn't expect answered.
New life. New plan.
Gadsden, Alabama—no blood ties, just strangers,
and still the same tired noise.
"What is she saying?"
Goddamn, can I breathe?
You claimed you were sick of me,
yet my name stayed busy in your mouth.
Calls came in—old connections, familiar voices—
and for a moment, peace touched down.
Then I chose myself.
Education. Forward motion.
Trade school should've been clean ground.
Instead, there you were again...
a church woman from Victory Headquarters,
passing rumors like communion.
Things you "heard."
Nothing true.
Blood don't make you holy.

Truth does.
You called me a thief because money owned you,
then demanded the title "grandma" like it was owed.
We family, right?
Please.
I learned early:
in the South, smiles cut deeper than knives,
and kinship is just another word people use
when they don't want to tell the truth.
And the truth is—
I survived you.

CHAPTER 12 — CONSEQUENCES

Down here, trauma don't knock...

It gets handed down like cast-iron skillets and last names.

Passed from elder to uncle, from auntie to silence,

seasoned with scripture and shame.

I learned early that healing wasn't encouraged;

it was suspicious.

I remember sitting in that mental health center,

the air stale, the carpet thin,

Mrs. Patricia Wynn being the only place I could lay my truth down

without it being turned into a weapon.

That room was my only safe porch.

The only place I could breathe.

Didn't know my grandmother's ears

were always pressed to the wall of my life.

Didn't know every word I said

was already sentenced before I left the chair.

Jesus—the way my chest locked up.

That'll give a person a "chip on their shoulder,"

but they call it anger so they don't have to call it survival.

"She crazy."

"She got problems."

No—I'm just done swallowing everybody else's rot.
I was never allowed to speak.
Every time I tried, they reduced me
to a used condom and a baby maker,
like morality only applies downward.
Judged by women who cheated freely,
collected baby daddies like scars,
then prayed loud for me to change.
That prayer was a joke.
A cruel one.
The whole town knowing your name
because of the clowns you protect—
a psycho boyfriend,
a son wrecked by dope and streets,
and somehow I'm the stain.
I kept walking anyway.
Gadsden, Alabama.
Bare feet on hot ground,
working, moving, surviving.
Hated by blood that never bled for me.
Trade school was a doorway.
Pregnancy slammed it shut.
And then the sentence came:
"That baby ain't my grandson."
Funny how she forgot

she did her own daughter that way.
Forgot how cold that casket was.
Forgot what neglect looks like
when it finally stops breathing.
You separated me from my cousin
to "teach me a lesson."
Funny how the lesson was always isolation.
Funny how punishment always wore family's face.
Now I wonder why I ever lived in your mind
when all you did was waste my time.
Nobody spoke.
Not the programs.
Not the groups.
Not the people paid to notice.
You dressed yourself in glittered bullshit,
flies circling but nobody naming the smell.
Spilled dirt on my name like yours
wasn't barely buried beneath the porch.
You tell me to forgive.
Like you forgave no one.
Like you didn't lay down and birth children
you didn't want just to keep a man.
Like you didn't demand tolerance
for sins you never owned.
Married and still bitter.

Years deep and still leaking poison.
And I was supposed to carry my mama's sorrow,
her open-mouth cries at night,
her grief sitting heavy on my chest
before I even knew what grief was.
I heard things as a child.
Saw things.
Spirits, voices, weight in the air.
You called it prayer and covered it up.
Now you tell my story like gossip,
like folklore,
like I wasn't just a child trying to survive the unseen.
Blood don't mean nothing
when evil shares your last name.
You say "we family"
like it's a spell.
Like repetition makes it true.
At this point I believe you are chanting,
not loving.
They say it can't be me.
They always say that.
But this is my life.
This is the cold truth of it.
This is why I write —
because silence almost killed me,

and ink don't flinch.
But yeah...
We family, right.

CHAPTER 13 — DISTANCE

Down South, secrets don't disappear.

They ferment.

They sit in the heat behind pressed dresses and Bible verses,

waiting on the right child to notice.

That child was me.

Imagine knowing everything and still being told you know nothing.

Imagine carrying the weight of abortions whispered behind closed doors,

molestation passed between sons and sisters like a family disease,

and watching it all get turned away like a bad smell nobody wants to claim.

Imagine truth being treated like treason.

I was the granddaughter once cherished...

picked up, shown off, spoken over like a promise.

And still, they played in my face.

The lies you said I told never changed,

not like the men you had did.

Funny how my truth was unforgivable

but your sins came with amens.

You judged me because you saw something on me.

You called it a threat.

You called it anointing.
Either way, it made you nervous.
I tried to gather my sanity while growing a child,
battling the same person who helped create him.
No coverage.
No backup.
No side to stand on.
Just me begging God...
please pull me aside before I break.
But I swallowed my pride.
Stayed quiet.
Stayed pregnant.
Stayed thinking.
He was a bird-brained mama's boy,
soft-spoken until the spirit shifted.
Dangerous when it counted.
The day you pointed a gun at me
should've been the end of the story,
but fear don't come with instructions.
I didn't know where to begin,
only how to survive.
So I recycled.
Same patterns.
Same exits that never opened.
By twenty, I relearned silence like it was scripture.

"We family, right?"

But my name stayed in everybody's mouth.

"How the fuck she gonna raise a baby?"

asked people who never raised children,

only reputations.

Front and center for sins so abnormal

they had to be dressed up as tradition.

How are you still standing with all that guilt?

I'll tell you how...

a Bible, a prayer, and a loud enough voice to drown the screams.

"We still family, right?"

I call bullshit.

You can't fuck and suck your way to heaven

and think forgiveness just shows up.

Not when you keep hurting

your deceased daughter's children

like they owe you for surviving her.

I looked like something God buried

and you cursed me anyway.

Acted like I wouldn't notice.

Told yourself that's why I'd never be married,

like loneliness was a punishment

and not your inheritance.

"We family, right?"

You stayed on a roll I never signed up for.

I never wished death on you....
but some stories demand daylight.
This one does.
You told me to stay in a child's place.
Funny how that place was built
on blood, sweat, tears,
and stolen innocence.
Everybody got fed
but the children.
Some things need to be destroyed,
but you call it loyalty.
You call it family.
It's a curse—
especially when it comes
from the highest one at the church front.
Robes pressed.
Hands lifted.
Demons tucked neatly behind hallelujahs.
Yell it louder.
Sing it harder.
Clap till your palms ache.
I see you now.
Not the version you rehearsed...
the real one.
The reason.

And yeah...
We family, right.

CHAPTER 14 — THE NEIGHBORHOOD WATCHED ME

Down South, they'll call you a hoe

when really you were just fed to the wolves

and blamed for bleeding.

Imagine being me...

mind bent, spirit chewed up

by the same bloodline that sat pretty at tea time,

pinkies up, secrets tucked under lace tablecloths.

They played house while I carried the aftermath,

and still had the nerve to ask what was wrong with me.

I knew who stayed in the closet and who lived on the down-
low,

who liked jail because the streets gave him a second name

and a reason to feel important.

You crushed my spirit, told me to forgive,

then splashed mess in my face because I remembered.

How do you forgive your mama's mama

when she watched her own child try to escape

and shut the door anyway?

My mama gone now—cold, quiet, buried—

and you looked at me like I owed you peace.

That resentment you carry?
You passed it down like china you never used.
Church was your hiding place.
Your heaven.
While the men who broke things got to live full lives,
I was told to "get over it,"
like time erases what silence preserved.
I had a child.
So what?
I still did better than you ever did—
but it cost me.
The man I thought was my forever
turned out to be another lesson in disguise.
His mama swore I ruined his life
while he stayed creeping, texting, lying in the dark.
And I stayed longer than I should've,
wearing love like a bruise.
I remember calling you late at night,
telling you too much.
But don't get it twisted...
I know how to leave a man.
One never defined me
the way you had to cling to one to feel chosen.
Loneliness held me
until love knocked again, reckless and loud.

That knock came with a gun,
with police lights,
with me standing outside figuring it out
while the door closed behind me.
I repeated cycles.
Kept you nearby.
And sometimes I think...
as my grandmother, you should've ended me then,
so I wouldn't have to carry
the stench of everybody else's sins.
My child is innocent.
That part is sacred.
He doesn't know y'all...and that's mercy.
But to talk about his differences
like they're flaws?
If insanity needs inspecting,
start with the mirror you avoid.
His father chased a bigger life
and left me holding ours.
But even he knows this...
I deserve respect.
I almost bled out bringing life in,
and I'll never bow down to bitterness dressed as family.
And you...
jealous in ways only broken people get,

worried about who I love
while your own house leaks betrayal.
Funny how that works.
Crazy thing is,
we still called family, right?
My tears never got paid for
like everybody else's did.
But one day...
when some of these voices go quiet
and the tables finally clear...
peace might sit down at last.
And I won't be there serving tea.

CHAPTER 15 — TOO MUCH

Cold Names, Hot Lies, and a Southern Last Name

I still can't wrap my head around how we keep saying we family

while stepping clean around the elephant tearing the house apart.

Nobody ever named the chaos.

Nobody ever named the hush money, the favors, or the people paid to look the other way.

Down here, silence is currency.

My life was peaceful—

right up until it wasn't.

My baby's father came in tall and thin, all arrogance and noise,

but weak where it mattered most.

And I blame his mama for that.

She raised boys like trophies,

trained to be defended no matter the damage left behind.

A pit bull for breeding reputations,

snarling at anyone who threatened the illusion.

The audacity of her judging me

when she one step from a diaper

and still acting brand new—

that's wild.

But we family, right?

You blame me for the separation.

You ask why you can't see your grandson.

You act confused like memory ain't selective.

But we family, right?

Enabling-mouth, loud-talking,

never-wrong-about-her-son type.

I never been so embarrassed

to have given my child that last name.

Sims—please.

More like a movie set.

All fantasy, no accountability.

Dreams sold cheap while you paraded through your sons' personal messes

like it was entertainment.

You never protected me.

Not once.

Instead, you said,

"Oh, I know my son would never—"

Never what?

Never lie?

Never hurt?

Never destroy?

There must be too much noise in your head

from all the excuses you rehearsed.

You judged me like I was the problem,

like looks and loudness replace character.
A big body don't make anyone beautiful.
And truth be told, your son was barely decent
even when the lights were off and the lies were on.
 I regret opening my mouth.
I regret trusting words.
But I don't regret my son.
Not ever.
He doesn't know you like that—
and that alone gives me peace.
You only demand him when it's convenient.
When it looks good.
When it feeds appearances.
You don't want a relationship...
you want a prop.
This whole thing is a circus,
and you stay the ringmaster.
My name stays on your tongue
like something you can't spit out,
like evidence you wish never existed.
You defend him no matter what.
Golden child.
Golden excuse.
Golden shield.
Even when harm followed him like a shadow,

you stood in front and said, "Not my son."
That's a mind game.
A cruel one.
I'm glad I escaped that house of mirrors.
That hell dressed as family.
But yeah...
we family, right?
There's more.
Always is.
But I don't need to scream it anymore.
I don't have to explain.
I've been figuring things out on my own
long before anyone believed I could.
Bitter baby mama?
Nah.
I'm just clever.
Quiet doesn't mean weak.
Silence doesn't mean stuck.
That narrative you tried to write about me
never fit because it was built on lies.
And in all honesty...
the children you raised aren't proof of wisdom,
they're proof of what happens
when accountability never shows up.
Down South, we love to say "family"

like it's holy.
But sometimes it's just a word
used to excuse damage
and demand access you no longer deserve.
And that's the coldest truth of it all.

CHAPTER 16 — GOD KEPT ME

Imagine being me—

building a life with someone I thought was a man,

only to realize he was hollowed out by fear,

a boy stitched together with bravado and his mama's voice.

All that insecurity wearing muscle and mouth,

while I carried the weight of being everything—

lover, worker, mule, mother—

and still got blamed when the cart broke.

I tried.

Lord knows I tried.

Perfect girlfriend by Southern standards—

holding it down, holding him up,

holding a newborn while moving furniture, groceries, and burdens,

while his grown self slept like a king

in a house I kept standing.

That's the part folks don't tell—

how devotion turns into labor

when love ain't mutual.

Behind closed doors,

he stayed sneaking.

Texting every woman breathing,

encouraged by blood that should've checked him.
A brother whispering poison.
A family pretending ignorance.
And me—
living in a bedroom that felt like a courtroom
where I was always on trial.
Mama's boys never hold themselves accountable.
They outsource blame.
So I got called the "bitter baby mama."
That's rich.
I worked.
I lost jobs.
I lost sleep.
I lost myself—
but I'm bitter?
He weaponized his temper like it was a tradition.
Southern discipline twisted into control.
Used fear as punctuation after betrayal,
then turned his whole family into witnesses
against me.
And still—
I'm the problem.
How could I forget
being thrown out cold with our baby, six months old,
after already surviving in the basement of his mama's house—

a grown woman reduced to borrowed space.
A gun pulled where love should've lived.
Trust shattered so loud it echoed.
Love is a dangerous thing
when it's one-sided.
And don't you dare say I didn't love you
when I sacrificed everything—
my place, my pride, my plans—
to chase the dream of a two-parent household.
I left and came back for you.
Only to walk straight into a plan
written by cowards.
"How to Break Her."
That was the theme song.
And you played it well.
That's why paperwork started talking.
That's why child support became necessary.
Because responsibility don't show up on its own
in families where men are protected
and women are disposable.
You got called "the man."
but you never stood up to the real power in your life.
Couldn't even correct your mama
when she disrespected me in my face.
DNA tests whispered like threats—

as if I didn't know who stood in my room,
as if my body was a question mark.
But we family, right?
You cheated.
Left me carrying consequences
I had to learn to live with
while you paraded new flesh like trophies,
acting like you didn't have a son breathing somewhere,
waiting on you to grow up.
And still—
we family, right?
How broken do you have to be
to protect harm
and call it loyalty?
How sick do you have to be
to shield mess
and blame the one bleeding...
You act wounded because I called you what you are,
but you the one moving in shadows,
making private plays,
bragging loud to anybody who'll listen.
Clout don't clean blood off hands.
I poured my heart out
like a four-page letter nobody read.
Gave up my apartment.

Gave up security.
Gave up peace—
for a dream you never deserved.
You don't know me.
You only know the version
your son needed you to believe.
But truth got weight,
and that's why documents sit where they sit now.
Your name don't carry honor to me.
And if my son never knows you,
that's protection—not punishment.
I know the truth.
That's enough.
Seven extra lives brought into chaos,
called family,
called legacy,
while responsibility stayed missing.
You had better things to do...
but choosing to mess with me
turned out to be the worst mistake.
Down South, folks love to say we family
when they mean don't expose us.
They mean stay quiet.
They mean carry it alone.
But I'm done carrying.

Say it again if you want...
we family, right?
Because now the cold truth stands up on its own,
and it don't need permission to speak.

CHAPTER 17 — ALMOST

Bitter, They Said

Down here, they love to name you before they ever know you.

They called me the "bitter baby mama."

while he was tangled up in a whole other mess,

acting confused about loyalty like it was a foreign language.

Couldn't tend to me; couldn't even stand himself,

so every disagreement turned into a catfight he started

and swore I caused.

I stayed.

Not because he deserved it...

but because I wanted my son to wake up smiling.

Because peace for a child sometimes costs a woman her dignity.

Because being tolerated felt better than being erased.

And still they said I was bitter.

Truth is, I was sharp.

Full of knowing.

A diamond sitting in a row of dull knives.

That scares people who benefit from chaos.

His sister said it first.

Loud.

Confident.

Like projection, don't sweat through the pores.

She had her own history trailing behind her,

then fixed her mouth to judge me over child support

while staying tangled for fourteen years

with Birmingham's loudest problem on wheels.

Attention was her oxygen.

Another child came, another excuse followed...

and still, I was the bitter one.

Thirty-six going on fossil,

but age don't equal wisdom and never has.

She wasn't important—

just noisy.

Moral of the story?

Stay in your lane when you know your brother is hell-bent on legs.

They had a contract I was never shown...

not sisterhood, not friendship...

just minions guiding me toward fire

and calling it family.

Miss me with the bend-over respect.

If you want reverence, earn it.

My son is mine, not a bargaining chip,

not a talking point, not your redemption arc.

Your brother ain't shit.

Plain.

Simple.

No poetry needed.

Sometimes I wish for a do-over—not the child, never him—

but the moment before I ever let that walking wreckage touch my life.

What's done is done.

My baby is here, healthy, loved, and whole.

He is my joy.

I just wish his father wasn't proof

that some men are diseases you survive,

not partners you grow with.

So call me bitter if it helps you sleep.

I call myself free.

CHAPTER 18 — KINDNESS ATTRACTS CHAOS

Green Lights, Closed Doors

Down here, folks love to call themselves men

while standing real still behind their mama's shadow.

Saying they run things,

but every move got strings attached.

He wasn't leading nothing...

just performing,

a puppet nodding on command while she wore the pants

and called it family loyalty.

Funny how loud people get about manhood

when the math don't add up.

Four hundred and something a month

like that covers nosebleeds, checkups, school switches,

IEP meetings, long emails to boards that don't listen,

and nights sitting up advocating for a child

who needs more than excuses.

But somehow there was money for a flashy ride

and a woman screaming, "My man!" like she won a prize at a
county fair.

Yeah.

He your man.

Traffic-stop energy.
Green in public, yellow behind closed doors.
And imagine this—
every time he shuts his eyes,
he mad.
Not peaceful.
Not settled.
Just mad.
Because blocking someone don't erase memory,
and hiding pictures don't delete history.
You can feel when you're a placeholder.
Hate is loud, but love is quiet and buried.
Girl, that man don't love you.
He loves what hating me gives him—
a storyline, a distraction, a place to lay his guilt.
I walked away with grace and receipts.
You stepped in and became the floor mat.
But we family, right?
All I ever asked for was credit where it's due.
I'm a damn good mama—
that's not opinion; that's fact.
Mud or no mud, partner or not,
my son will never wonder, never want, never beg.
That's my promise.
That's my legacy.

Will he ever be present?

Probably not.

And honestly, I'm good.

I don't want to collapse under trauma

just to make somebody else feel included.

Enjoy what's left.

Leftovers come seasoned with history anyway.

He like to talk about bodies and weight

like genetics skipped his mama entirely.

But that's Southern irony for you...

Project loud; ignore mirrors.

Bitter?

Nah.

I was fed up.

Big difference.

So all you stalkers, enablers, and background commentators—

y'all can hush now.

This chapter closed clean,

and I didn't need permission to turn the page.

Just stay off my clit—I don't want to bump into another bitch.
Mmk.

CHAPTER 19 — WOMEN AND ENVY

I'll admit it—I wasn't always humble.

I came up spitfire, mean-mouthed, and king-cobra-quiet.

Classy, observant, watching everything while saying nothing.

It took time to grow into the woman I am now.

Back then?

I was a kid raised on survival.

You get used to getting hit; something switches off.

Pain turns into background noise.

They call that psycho—

I call it adaptation.

You could've left me alone.

I told you that.

Time passed, seasons turned, people changed—

but don't confuse growth with fear.

I'm not scared of you

or any watered-down mess you dipped into.

Let's be honest...

it was always about money.

Flash wrapped in empty promises,

children dressed like trophies,

bragging like that makes a man.

Pathetic.

Still—

that's how the cookie crumbles down here.

I'm a Southern belle by definition,

steel-spined, soft-spoken, unbreakable.

You never cracked me.

That's why I write... 🪨

because ink holds pain better than memory,

and lyrics outlive wasted time.

Sometimes I wonder if change ever comes.

It does.

Late.

Right on time.

Karma, don't rush.

She circles.

Quiet.

Then lands heavy.

Belt to truth, truth to tears.

If I were a fly on the wall,

I'd watch them fall like dice...

clean, undeniable.

But hey...

we family, right?

CHAPTER 20 — MONEY FROM GRIEF

Down South, knowing the truth don't always mean speaking
it.

Sometimes, it means learning how to play dumb

while time flies and receipts stack quiet.

I watched scholars come and go,

polished titles and pressed smiles,

all stopping by to see the woman they called "Mom."

I watched them help clean up messes,

smooth over stories,

erase what was already worn thin from overuse.

That's where I drew the line.

Because erasing history don't heal it—

it just makes liars comfortable.

Mrs. Hamburger—my dearest aunt—

the front you keep could win awards.

You helped my grandmother reach into money

that never belonged to her.

You called it "resources."

Settlement money.

Mine and my sister's...

placed into hands that never planned to return it.

Spent on sorrow and excuses,

then tossed back at us like gratitude should be enough.
We got nothing.
And when I spoke my truth,
you looked at me like I was less than.
Girl, wake up.
Pushing seventy and still bitter to the bone,
dry with resentment,
backed up with secrets that spoil everything they touch.
You mixed blood money with bravado,
Hennessy's confidence and quiet targeting,
then aimed it at me like I wouldn't notice.
Your networks stretch wide,
friends everywhere,
stories planted neat—but if something smells off,
it ain't me.
Old Southern saying...
before you check someone else,
make sure your own mess ain't leaking.
Careful.
Age don't stop spills.
I watched the halls fill with walkers and whispers,
dentures clacking, memories dancing loose.
I wondered if the last hit life gave you
rattled something you never fixed.
You didn't envy me...

you spat at me.

Like I was a roach from a crack you pretended not to have.

Funny thing about knowledge...

it don't mean clarity.

Even the learned need assistance

when they refuse to look down.

And still—

we family, right?

I saw the disgust.

Heard the plans.

Private payments, quiet signatures,

leases handed to squatters,

all to keep a broken house standing

and call it a strategy.

You never cared...

and I don't know why you pretend to now.

Especially when my grandmother nearly dried out after surgery,

care delayed, concern selective.

You only guarded what was yours.

Truth be told, your distance did more good than harm.

You talked bad about my uncle,

said he caused your daughter's mess,

like curses don't pass themselves down.

Blessings don't come from lessons you refuse to learn.

Meanwhile, the skeletons danced hard,

and you thought I forgot we all had a hand in it.

Mrs. Perfect.

Mrs. All That.

Mrs. Doctor.

A woman who moves only for her own blood,

lifting her chin high

when it should've been lowered to face the truth, she stepped
in.

I never got a pass…

just the same chorus: she lying, she lying,

said over and over about a living body

treated like a corpse.

Funny how quick y'all were to call me

when you needed something.

How precious that grandchild became then.

How easy it was to move hours away for "more,"

leaving responsibility behind.

Tell the truth.

Stop playing dirty.

We family… girl, just get the raid and spray all the pests… like
you do undercover at best…

 but I'm tired of the exaggerations,

the whispers, the backroom deals.

You move like rats searching for cheese,

never still, never honest.

But hey…

we family, right?
Snakes don't hiss.
They don't announce.
They slide quiet,
counting on you not to feel the cold
until it's already wrapped around the truth.

CHAPTER 21 — NO SAFE ROOM

Down here, we say kids grow fast,
but the truth is some of us never got to be kids at all.
We learned too early how to watch faces change
when money waved,
how love bent depending on who was looking.
Raised by a woman with a hoarder's house
and a colorist's heart—
two-faced, shifting like heat off asphalt.
Tragic, really.
But we family, right?
Golightly—that's the name.
Ain't nothing light about it.
Bold, yes.
But heavy with history.
Names changed like seasons,
men came and went,
children misplaced in memory,
yet everybody clutched a Bible tight
when death crept close enough to whisper.
You said you loved me and my sister,
but love in that house had conditions.

Shade mattered.

Tone mattered.

Fairness never did.

My sister, Leah—

Lord, she carried more than a child should.

Her scalp inflamed, her pain mocked.

Haircut not with care but cruelty.

A brush turned weapon.

And when we wanted to feel pretty...

just once—

you stomped it flat like it offended you.

I couldn't stay quiet.

Rebellion was the only language left.

Not that you cared.

Hell never flinched in that house.

I used to wish our mama was still breathing.

That wish stayed lodged in my throat.

You drove us to the edges,

especially Leah.

So desperate to be seen

that at seven years old

she spelled "HELP" with her own shit... the only way she knew
how.

That should've stopped the world.

It didn't.

You only paid attention when we were no longer little—

when innocence started to look like something to manage,
something to control.
Doctors spoke.
Warnings were given.
You ignored them all.
Instead, you lied.
Blamed me.
You always had a twist ready
when the spill was yours.
When truth mattered most,
you disappeared behind excuses.
And all I ever wanted—
was honesty.
You judged me harder than anyone ever should.
Cold.
Final.
Like you weren't the architect of the damage.
I swore then...
I would never put my child through that kind of misery.
Never recycle that poison and call it family.
Because that house wasn't a home... I say burn the
motherfucker down because ...
it was a horror show.
And you, my uncles, and a few others
should've been written out of the script entirely.
Cast away.

Departed.

Strangers by choice.

Blood ain't thicker than water.

Not when it dripped down my body,

not when I had to scrub it off myself

and keep breathing like nothing happened.

Down South, folks protect legacies.

I chose survival.

And that choice still stands...

Ask God for forgiveness, just like you used to tell me, or shove it down my throat of uncertain warranty... guilt and shame beating that ass, and red all over. I never wanted to be in the loop, but y'all brought me into it like a dented, dried four-leaf clover.

CHAPTER 22 — SPIRITUAL WARFARE

Blood Ain't a Blindfold.

Cold Truths Don't Sweat

Down South, secrets don't hide.

They just sit longer.

And when folks finally speak, they act like the truth betrayed them.

Since we airing things out, here's one I carried quiet.

My aunt Cole liked to pretend she cared.

Liked the performance of the concern more than the work of it.

She locked my mother's brother into a promise

with words she never planned to keep,

then crossed the line with someone he trusted.

That kind of betrayal don't just bruise a man...

it rewrites him.

She called herself complicated.

Said parts of her were hidden.

But hiding ain't the same as healing,

and pain don't give anyone permission

to tear others apart and call it love.

What always chilled me

was how quick she turned desperation into manipulation.

Threats dressed as vulnerability.
"I can't live without you"
said not in love, but in control.
Two children brought into a house
where affection was rationed,
earned, withheld.
That's not intimacy—that's leverage.
Roles stayed twisted.
Responsibility shifted.
And while order pretended to exist,
truth leaked out the sides...
quiet infidelity, louder denial.
Chaos always finds a way to announce itself.
She had a talent for stirring mess
and then stepping back like she didn't light the match.
A sharp voice.
No patience.
No softness for children,
only rules and resentment.
Motherhood reduced to authority,
never care.
The line that ended everything for me
was how she treated my child and me...
like we were something to be sanitized away,
feared instead of understood.

Jealousy wrapped in judgment
is still jealousy,
no matter how you justify it.
Now she sits beside a man
who learned survival looks like silence.
He drinks.
He rages.
Walls remember what mouths deny.
And still they stand together,
calling it marriage,
calling it family.
Money moved where it shouldn't have.
Lies told clean and deliberate.
Brothers misled.
Truth postponed.
And when consequences finally knocked,
the old chant came back—
"she lying, she lying."
Funny how recordings change stories.
Funny how accountability shows up
right when denial runs out of room.
Twelve years deep in a union built on fear and smoke,
one owning, one enduring,
both pretending this is what commitment looks like.
Some secrets stay locked not from shame,

but from terror of being known.
And still...
when the dust settles,
when voices crack,
when blame gets passed around like communion...
someone always says it.
"We family, right?"
Down here, that phrase gets used
to excuse what should've ended long ago.
But blood don't sanctify harm,
and silence don't make lies holy.
Cold truth is this:
family that feeds on damage
will eventually choke on it.
And I'm done pretending
I don't see the mess
just to keep the peace.
Definitely should've left me tf alone.

CHAPTER 23 — PRIVATE PRAYERS

Down where the clay sticks to your boots and the heat don't forgive, there lived an uncle they called Junior, though nothing about him ever grew up. Born with a borrowed name and a borrowed spine, he spent his whole life ducking shadows and calling it wisdom. Folks said a man earns his weight in this world by standing still when the wind comes. Junior always leaned.

He never learned the heft of courage, never learned how to plant his feet. He learned how to smile thin, how to trade blood for pocket change. Sold his own daughter's trust for something cheap and soft, like it might mold him into a better man if he just pressed hard enough. Then he wrapped himself in talk like a preacher wraps sin, calling himself chosen and calling himself untouchable.

"Who are you?" he barked once at his own kin, puffed up like a bullfrog in a drought. "You can't step to me."

Step to what, exactly? A man who burned his mind chasing fumes and called it insight? A ghost who kept changing towns because mirrors remembered him better than people did? It was hard to tell which version of him showed up that day, but none of them stood straight.

He paraded lies like Sunday clothes, arm in arm with a woman who wore another face every time the truth walked by. Wig crooked, paint too red, pretending royalty while dipping into an old woman's purse like it was found money. Lottery luck is built on borrowed grief. And Junior grinned beside her, proud as if the whole thing weren't stitched together with betrayal.

He made loud threats to hide quiet shame. He kept friends close who'd already crossed him and kept secrets everyone else could smell. Talked about loyalty while standing knee-deep in treachery. Talked about manhood like it was something you could rent for the afternoon and return before dark.

"Family," he said. That's what this all was. Family is like a locked room, like a bad inheritance, like a name you keep even when it rots your mouth to say it.

Until

His mother lay cold beneath red dirt... and he had reinvented himself over eight hours, pretending the past didn't know the way home. But the South remembers. The ground remembers. You can't ghost your way out of a life you already lived.

So yeah—Junior was something, all right. Just not what he ever claimed to be.

CHAPTER 24 — DISCERNMENT

Understood. Colder means quiet, not loud. No heat. No mercy. Just truth laid out like frost.

By the time I knew his face, I already knew to keep distance. Some people don't need introductions—your body learns them before your mind does.

He was my uncle in the way rust belongs to iron. Same origin. Different outcome. The streets had names for him. None of them kind. None of them wrong. He moved through life thin and trembling, always reaching, never holding on. Whatever he touched came away lighter. Whoever trusted him learned better.

He prayed out loud and ruined things in private. That was his pattern. Always a sermon. Always a wreck. He carried hatred for his mother like it was oxygen, even while breathing on her mercy. That contradiction defined him better than any story he told about himself.

What he did fractured the family long before the house came apart. Some acts don't break bones; they break timelines. After that, care became unnecessary. Distance became instinct. You don't grieve what teaches you to stay alert.

He drifted. New rooms. New women. Same emptiness. Built replacement families out of people just as lost, living in places meant to be temporary but somehow never were. He called it survival. It looked more like erosion.

He liked to play dangerous. Liked to feel important. Twice, he traded my name for approval, the way a man trades loose change for one more roll of the dice. Loyalty was never in his pocket long enough to spend.

My grandmother tried to save what was already gone. Love does that sometimes—it refuses to update itself. He repaid her by stripping the house down to its bones, pulling value from the walls like it owed him. Shelter turned into currency. Memory turned into debt.

Violence followed him, but not the kind that makes legends. The small kind. The inevitable kind. The kind that comes from strangers who recognize instability faster than kin ever wants to admit. Consequences dressed as coincidence.

I don't wish him harm. I don't need to. He lives inside the outcome of his own choices. That's colder than anger. That's permanent.

We share blood. Nothing else. He is not my past, and he is not my future. He is a lesson that stands still while I keep walking.

And that's the end of it.

CHAPTER 25 — SILENT STRENGTH

All dirty laundry stank no matter how much you wash it, but
...

I was born in a place where the air sticks to your skin and family sticks worse. Down here, blood don't mean love—it mean obligation, and obligation is the sharpest knife a person can hand you and still swear they care. I learned early that being "family" meant being drafted into messes I never made, carrying sins that weren't mine, and being told to hush while my life got picked apart like a chicken on Sunday.

They always said to stay in a child's place. Said it loud. Said it often. Said it when I spoke truth, said it when I bled, and said it when I asked why everything bad somehow landed in my lap. "Know your place," they'd say, as if humility was something you beat into somebody instead of something you earn. They called it love. I call it training a mule to walk into fire.

I was fed to the wolves early. Not even starving wolves—just greedy ones. Folks who already had enough but wanted what little breath I had left. All this hell over some cartoon-laughing, church-hat-wearing grandmother drama, like Looney Tunes running on a loop, except nothing's funny when the punchline is your life. They set the trap house up with sin stacked to the ceiling and blood running down my legs and stood back watching, saying, "That's family."

Family don't look like that to me.

Family don't jump you from all sides while calling it concern. Family don't rob you of time, dignity, and peace, then ask why you tired. What y'all gave me wasn't love—it was vinegar and oil, and you kept shaking the bottle, mad it wouldn't blend.

It started with loose mouths and hellhound calls, summoned trouble like it was tradition. One lie turned into ten, ten into a meeting, and a meeting into everybody suddenly knowing my business better than I did. You read my line while I was trying to restart my life, rebuild what you helped burn down. You didn't have the time to help me heal, but you sure had time to assume I wouldn't notice when you crossed me.

I noticed.

I noticed when I was the one driving out of state, burning gas and patience, catching tickets for somebody else's chaos. I noticed when y'all said, "She won't say nothing," like silence was my natural role. I noticed how easy it was for you to gamble with my safety but clutch your own comfort like scripture.

Truth is, I sat with the thought of walking away. Thought about saying, "Forget everybody," the same way everybody forgot me. But some cousins—bless them—whispered in my ear and told me it wasn't worth it, told me to keep my soul clean even if the room was filthy. I listened. And that's the part that still stings.

My heart turned into a nest of wasps. Every memory is a sting. Every conversation is another welt. And still, you said "family," like the word alone should bandage the wound.

My testimony didn't matter. My pain was inconvenient. Instead, you propped up the loudest, highest, most self-righteous voice in the room—somebody who preached about humbling people while refusing to humble her own demons. Married money, worshipped power, and demanded silence from me like I was a pet, a lapdog, or a corner girl meant to be grateful for scraps.

I'm tired.

Tired of being pulled into fights over property, over scraps, over things you'd snatch back the moment it suited you. "Indian giver" love. Conditional loyalty. Smiles with receipts attached. You spit on the woman who gave me life, the one lying cold now, bones and dust and memory, and expected me to clap along. You never sacrificed for her. Never bled for her. But you sure used her name when it fit your story.

I loved once, too. Deep. Respectful. For years. And you chipped at it. One insult, one dismissal, one excuse for a man smaller than his fists, a man who raised hands instead of character. You let that slide. You always let that slide. Something is wrong with that.

Money made you feel rich, but all I ever saw was bought minds and rented morals. Shiny on the outside, hollow where the truth should live.

If my mama had lived to see this, if God hadn't swept her away before y'all finished what you started, things would've been different. I know that in my bones. But she's gone, and you hide behind that absence like it absolves you.

And still you say, "We family."

Yeah.

But when?

Because from where I stand, family ain't supposed to feel like a sentence. Family ain't supposed to cost you your voice, your body, or your sanity. Family ain't supposed to watch you drown and argue about who owns the water.

I survived you. And that might be the truest thing I'll ever say.

CHAPTER 26 — WATCHING CONSEQUENCES

Down South, the heat don't just sit on your skin—it presses into your bones, makes secrets sweat out whether you ready or not. Folks say blood is thicker than water, but they never tell you blood can drown you too.

They called it family.

That word came wrapped in Sunday manners and rotted underneath. Came with casseroles and curses, with smiles sharp enough to skin you alive. They said it while speaking about my disabled child like he was contamination, like God made a mistake and forgot to clean it up. Funny how the cruel are always scared of sickness but never scared of themselves.

What's worse than hate is how ordinary they made it.

Like it was normal.

Like cruelty was just another heirloom passed down with the land.

They laughed. Others looked away. Wrong got cheered like a hometown win and praised loud and proud, while truth got buried behind the barn. Down here, folks clap hardest when the devil wears a familiar face. They call it loyalty. Call it love. Call it family.

I call it rot.

I was told to shut my mouth so many times I learned how to bleed quiet. Every time I spoke, they said I was lying. Every time I stayed silent, they said I was guilty. Witnesses watched—some dead now, some disappeared into distance and drink. Plenty are still breathing but too scared to pick up the phone. Silence is the South's favorite alibi.

They want closure now.

But closure is for people who ever opened the door.

I never got that.

All I got was hands, words, and orders. Bend. Take it. Be grateful. Be quiet. Be family. Exposure terrifies them because light don't negotiate; it reveals. And blood, once seen, don't wash out.

They should fear exposure.

God already knows.

They walk around baptized in performance, saying hallelujah with mouths still wet from harm. They think heaven got a back room for folks like them. But heaven don't want what hell already claimed. You can't pray over spilled innocence and call it clean. You can't sing louder than the screams you caused.

And they know it.

That's why they need me silent.

They wanted me folded, compliant, useful. Wanted me bent over tradition like it was holy. Wanted me to wear the family name like a brand on my back. But to be born from me and still demand my obedience, to be kin and still poison my child...that ain't love. That's possession.

I couldn't stomach it anymore.

Too vile.

Too familiar.

You can't expect pigs raised on filth to smell themselves, but don't be shocked when they bite. Imagine learning your own grandmother was a voice carried nationwide, preaching righteousness while playing crazy in private. Imagine contracts signed, papers legal, truth stamped and witnessed—only for her to say you tricked her. Baby, lies shake when truth stands long enough.

Years they smiled.

Years they got away.

Years they bled us quiet and thanked God afterward.

My sister and I...nosebleeds, prayers, and locked doors. The town whispered. They always do. Folks say it must be hard being talked about. They don't know what it's like to live inside a story where survival is the only sacrament. I swallowed pride, swallowed shame, swallowed worse just to hide the bruises that would've embarrassed them.

They say we family.

No.

I was born into a curse wearing love's face. A Southern inheritance where help comes from strangers and harm comes from blood. Where loyalty is demanded, not earned. Where children pay for sins they didn't commit and abusers call it God's will.

So I picked up a pen and paper.

Because the written word don't flinch.

Because justice moves slow, but it remembers.

Because Hell hates witnesses.

This ain't a sad story.

This is a record.

And blood don't lie because, again, the curse they always chant... We family, right, and that don't mean a damn thing ...

CHAPTER 27 — NO REVENGE

They say the South remembers everything.

Dirt remembers boots.

Porches remember arguments.

Women remember what they survived.

Imagine being me.

Twenties still green, still believing blood meant loyalty and love meant endurance. Down here they teach you early: hold on, even when holding on burns your palms raw. Especially then.

I had a baby on my hip and a war at my feet. A newborn with lungs strong enough to shake the trailer walls and a man-child clinging to his mama's breath like it was oxygen she invented. She strutted her stink through every room, bragging loud about cars that weren't paid for and a son who couldn't stand upright without her spine pressed into his back. In her mind, that was something to be proud of.

The dance between me and my baby's father could've made the evening news. Not love—no—combat. A duel with no referee and plenty of witnesses who pretended not to see it. He sang promises at night like hymns, but they were never meant for me. They floated down highways toward Birmingham rooms with rented smiles and borrowed names.

Meanwhile, my love burned quiet and steady, the way wood stoves do—no spectacle, just heat that keeps a child alive.

They called me bitter.

Funny word, 'bitter.' It comes easy from mouths that never swallowed what I did. He handed me sickness like it was nothing and then watched the world turn around and call me "dirty." That kind of thing brands you. You don't forget it. You carry it in your bones while folks swear you're the problem for remembering it.

I left.

I came back.

Because down here they whisper curses in the same breath as family.

We family, right?

No.

This ain't a dollhouse.

This was an innocent soul breathing beside me.

Every time I fell, I showed up anyway. Fed him. Bathed him. Loved him out loud. And still he called me a pathetic excuse for a mother while never lifting a finger for our son's care. The baby's cries scraped his nerves raw, but my exhaustion was invisible. Somehow, I was still the bitter one.

He laughed at thrift-store clothes, like dignity had a price tag. Didn't matter that I washed them clean and pressed them sharp. My baby looked fly because love tailors better than money ever could.

He called the police when I tried to leave. Said I was the problem while blocking the door. Said escape looked like aggression when it wasn't his idea.

Love died slow, like a song played wrong too many times. Sex couldn't save it—not even when it was good—because hunger ain't intimacy. I cooked. Cleaned. Ironed. Listened. Healed. Hustled. Filed paperwork. Held everybody together with shaking hands. But his mama said no—not her son. I ruined his life, she said, while he put a bullet through mine and our child's future with one pull of the trigger called neglect.

He kept me boxed in—him, his other woman, and his mother—then got mad when I showed up standing tall, claiming my place, trying to end the mess like an adult. He was embarrassed.

Imagine how I felt.

I never tried to even the score. The South notices that, too.

Now he flashes a new love dressed in money and calls it "success." Funny how fast folks forget who warmed them when they were cold. Funny how silence feels like victory when you've been excused your whole life.

They gossiped about me like it was currency. Told stories in barbershops and laughed about hands laid on me, bruises hidden under sleeves. But the walls remember. Hallways remember. Blood remembers.

He once talked about giving our son away to dodge responsibility. Said it like it was practical. Like fatherhood was optional. Now the boy's face mirrors his, and I wonder if that reflection ever costs him sleep.

Probably not.

They still say I'm bitter.

But bitterness is just truth that won't sweeten itself for liars.

I know my worth now. Know how low a man has to be to make a woman forget hers. I won't shrink myself again for someone who needed permission to be decent.

The South remembers everything.

And one day, so will my son.

Definitely don't have to explain because absence and pictures say a thousand words that fake smiles could never hold up to.

CHAPTER 28 — ENDING THE LINE

Down South, blame travels faster than truth.

They told me I chose wrong.

Grandma said it.

Uncles nodded.

Everybody with a hand in my dough had an opinion about my life like they financed it clean.

"She chose wrong," they said,

like single motherhood was a sin she invented

and not a road my grandma herself walked...

only difference was she had help

and time softened the story once the kids grew up and looked successful enough to forgive her past.

But when it was me?

They called it consequence.

Don't turn my son into a charity case so you can polish your conscience. Don't disappear, then come back with grocery bags and expect applause. You said it yourself—on the phone, bright as day.

"That's what she get. I hope her ass struggles the rest of her life."

That curse still echoes in my chest.

And then there were the secrets.

Down here, secrets rot slow and stink forever.

The kind that involves children and silence and grown folks who clap for monsters instead of protecting babies. My mother high-fived a man who stole something he had no right to touch and said, "That's what you get."

I carry that sentence like a scar I never asked for.

They wonder why I don't answer calls.

Why I don't want apologies that come late and hollow.

"I'm sorry," they say—

sorry the way people are sorry they got caught,

not sorry they did it.

I learned how to be strong from cousins who stood tall, upper-class, polished, and composed. They taught me posture and quiet pride. But even they don't know the weight I've swallowed to stay silent this long. I'm making noise now because this hurt buried me alive for years.

I grieved for a family that never loved me right.

Grieved the idea of normal.

Got hurt from both sides and kept standing, wondering what hell was next.

Next came kin with fake titles...real estate managers from friends of friends...swearing blood loyalty while slipping knives into paperwork. Taxes altered. Documents shifted. Dirt under fingernails, pretending to be business. I watched my stability get stolen clean, like theft done in Sunday clothes.

Why was I born into this?

You never liked me. You never hid it well. That's why I scatter at the first whiff of y'all, like prey that learned the sound of danger early.

You'll never tell them how you called housing authorities, sent emails under company names, or pulled strings just to watch me fall. How Constantine Homes became another chapter in your quiet cruelty. Homelessness wasn't an accident... It was a plan.

What do you want from me?

My blood already paid the rent.

Grandma plays sweet and forgetful now. Says forgiveness fixes everything. Wants phone calls and holidays and pretending. But I remember the tricks, the silence, the way survival was always my responsibility alone.

"Forgive and forget," they say.

I won't.

I don't feed dogs piss-poor food, and I don't feed lies to broken hearts anymore either. You hated me while asking me to help save her from dying by her own hand. You needed me but never respected me. That contradiction tells me everything.

And the gossip...Lord, the gossip. Counting men between my thighs like it's church business. Warning others I'll steal husbands while ignoring the marriages you tried to ruin, the reason folks packed up and left town in the first place.

Funerals always beg unity.

I cover my face instead.

A black widow dressed in truth.

I have no sympathy left.

Neither did you.

Down South, the soil remembers everything.

And one day, so will I—

without shame,

without silence,
and without you...
But again, we family, right?

CHAPTER 29 — FOR MY MOTHER

The South remembers everything.

Even when folks swear it don't.

I was raised where the night hums like a wound that won't close, owls and grasshoppers crying louder than the truth, and the moon hanging low like it got business in our suffering. They don't tell you this part in the church songs. They just clap on beat and call it family.

You never knew how many nights I cried in the dark.

Rocking my baby slow like time itself might break if I moved too fast.

My tears was the moonlight, shining straight down on my son's face, and I kept whispering, "Jesus loves me, this I know," not because I felt it...but because I needed something holy enough to erase what y'all did to me.

They love that word, family.

They chant it like a spell, like it cleans blood off the floorboards.

But family don't do shit like that.

What y'all was, was enemies with familiar faces—energy harvesters smiling through Sunday teeth.

The brick walls saw me.

That's the part nobody argues with.

Those walls held me back night and day, listened when I talked to God in a voice so low it scared even me. I told Him everything. Every name. Every memory. Every silence I swallowed so other people could eat steak while I was expected to drink piss and say, "Thank you."

See, the South knows about bones left out.

Knows how one small thing can slip and crack a whole soul open.

Mine slid right out of me somewhere between girlhood and survival. I wished—Lord, I wished—I never came from a timeline tied to y'all. Would've sold the whole bloodline if that were an option.

They like to act righteous.

Praise and worship on Sunday, secrets buried Monday through Saturday.

Abortions hid behind hymns.

Pregnancies were blamed on me before I even knew my body was a battlefield.

Birth control early, shame even earlier.

"She gon' get pregnant young," they said.

I didn't.

You did.

And the eldest sister swept it up neat, like strategy, like it was just another mess on the kitchen floor.

You fixed your mouth on me for years.

Bent the truth till it snapped.

But time don't stay bent forever.

A few more years and my trauma won't sound like a sad song; it'll sound like a testimony folks choke on.

I ain't silent no more.

That's the chef's kiss.

Everything documented. Calls logged. Cops driving miles just to clear smoke you laughed through. As a kid, every officer knew your name, but you played it cute. You always do.

Golightly.

Bell.

Grant.

Amos.

Southern names, heavy as headstones.

You lived comfortable off sacrifices you won't ever confess. My mother's blood. My own leaking spirit. I am becoming a woman in the middle of your sins. That's the part you won't tell.

God gave me ancestral strength, and I carry it like a blade wrapped in scripture. I'm sorry I was even gifted to y'all—because not once did you try to set me free. Not then. Not now.

When the day comes and they dress you in blue on blue, I hope it ain't cold.

Hope it ain't snowing.

I'll remember the good parts, sure... But most memories smell like iron. And around here, baby blood get rinsed easy. Too easy.

The South remembers.

And now...so do I.

CHAPTER 30 — FOR MY SISTER

The South got a way of freezing you without snow.

Cold mornings where gratitude and grief sit at the same table, not speaking, just staring at each other like they kin but don't trust it. That's where my story learned to breathe.

I give credit where credit due...because even a cracked cup can still hold water.

Mrs. Hamburger and her lonely slice of cheese, separated now, living in different houses and different versions of the truth—I still thank them. For the small kindnesses. The kind you don't notice till you're starving for them. My cousin Nita and her family too. Blood that didn't turn their back all the way. Blessed and highly favored—that's what I call it, even when the blessing came wrapped in strangers. Thank you for proper education and even a bath and a few laughs ...

Strangers matter in the South.

A piece of chewing gum passed hand to hand like communion.

They called it Widsom...misspelled maybe, but it stuck.

Kept my mouth busy when my thoughts wanted to chew me alive.

Gadsden shelters held me when the world wouldn't.

Yeah, the bedbugs ate me alive and left their prayers all over my skin, but y'all fed me nourishment that kept my mind from rotting. There's a difference between being clean and being spiritually clean, and somehow I walked out with the second one intact.

Hillcrest mental health...patient, like winter sun, weak but still showed up.

I remember the warmth of voices when I was cracking down the middle.

Every warm meal.

Every cotton-woven outfit that didn't ask where I came from.

Those were gifts. Real ones.

And the □ hugs... Lord, the hugs y'all never knew I needed. I held my head high off borrowed strength, and that says more than pride ever could.

Family beef ain't loud at first.

It's quiet.

It's death dressed up as memory.

It's grieving what you never thought would hurt you... until that's all you got left.

Now it's just me, my kid, no husband, and a little baby sister I adore like the last light on a long road. I'm glad I still got you. The pain still itches, but it don't bleed like it used to.

Days pass like an anime series...episodes full of battles nobody sees, lessons wrapped in color, and survival disguised as entertainment. I hope it inspires somebody. I really do.

Every conversation I've had, I keep it.

Tuck it away like canned food for the soul.

That's enough for me.

I love the ones that love me.

Simple math. Southern math.

This didn't break me, though it almost did. Had me bent so low I could hear the earth breathing. But God knows how to make everything shake without letting it fall apart completely.

Words got power in the tongue, they say.

But mine live in the pen.

Ink tracing every curve of muscle I tried to protect with dignity.

Writing is how I stay standing.

"We family, right?"

Maybe.

Maybe not.

Either way, I'm still here.

Still willing.

Still surviving.

And that kind of cold don't kill you.

It sharpens you... But again, we family, right?

Either way it's my delight...

CHAPTER 31 — FOR THE SILENT

The South teaches you early how to tell what's real and what's just noise.

How to feel the difference between a front porch smile and a heart that truly means well. I learned that lesson the long way, through silence and separation, through stories that weren't mine to carry but somehow landed in my hands anyway.

There are two women I hold gently in my spirit—my sister Leah and my cousin Tyana. We were kept apart by other people's lies, by the weight of sins that never belonged to us. Still, I see you. Even when you didn't know how to begin telling your own stories, even when the words stayed caught in your throats, your lives spoke for you.

It was hard to witness from a distance. Hard, but holy.

And I'm grateful—truly grateful—that joy found you after I was removed from that house of harm, that place dressed up as family but built on ruin. God has a way of redirecting footsteps, and when He did, He gave me something rich: the knowing that I gained an angel watching over me when He aligned my path with yours.

That matters.

I still call. I still check in. Not out of obligation, but because you matter. Every laugh we share now fills in the gaps where time was stolen. Every smile makes up for memories that never got the chance to form. Even with all the spice...extra heat from a complicated past...we move with grace. We always seem to find our way back to one accord.

That's Southern sisterhood.

Not loud. Not forced.

Just steady. Loyal. Rooted.

I love that you both move with maturity...in mind and in spirit. There's something beautiful about women who survive without letting bitterness harden them. Being blessed isn't about an easy life; it's about God's kiss on the forehead, anointing you to stand anyway. To live well anyway. To prove, quietly and consistently, that curses don't get the final say.

We are still here.

Still connected.

Still choosing love.

And in the South, that kind of bond is legacy.

CHAPTER 32 — TOUCH NOT

I was born knowing "thank you" before I knew "please."

That's a Southern thing.

You learn gratitude early, like learning which boards on the porch will break if you step wrong.

I ain't a saint.

Never claimed to be.

Saints don't survive long where I come from.

I've said "bitch" before...said it plain and meant it...about a woman bent low for money, pride left somewhere between the knees and the need. Folks like to pretend words are worse than what made them necessary. I don't. I call things what they are.

I once snatched a mailbox, too.

Not out of rage—out of irony.

They welcomed me into a house I paid for with school money, smiling wide like hospitality was free. Cost them nothing. Gave me everything I didn't ask for: mutant roaches bold enough to look you in the eye, toilets that never worked, rats with the run of the place. But still—we family, right?

Funny how family sit warm with generators humming while deeds get altered in quiet rooms. Then they call you crazy for noticing. Should've handled your own mama with that same concern, but again—we family, right?

Lies pass through bloodlines like bad hymns.

A lease pulled out of a dirty place by a corrupted uncle—brother—whatever title helps him sleep. He stay singing that Bone Thugs cry, mourning everything except what he actually did. I used to love that music. Now it just remind me how grief get rehearsed while harm stays real.

You, the baby uncle, still throwing fits and still suckling sour buttermilk titties like accountability never weaned you. Don't even call your own daddy—money ghosts you never earned but stay mad you never got. That part shameful.

But shame don't stop mouths.

You spoke on my child with a mouth rotted by a burnt-back tooth. Had the nerve.

Maybe keep your lavender marriage tucked where you hide the rest of the truth. Calling survival "love" don't make it holy—it just make it quiet. But still—we family, right?

The coldest thing you ever said was about my grandma.

Waiting on her decline like a calendar date, already planning the nursing home. That's when I learned how easy it is for y'all to throw people away. Houses too. Glass ones, mostly. Shatter loud, then act surprised by the noise.

I don't throw.

I watch.

I watch brothers-in-law pay taxes under "Mrs. Hamburger" emails. I watch names change, stories shift, blame migrate. It's almost impressive—the creativity of corruption. Almost.

But I stay grateful.

Grateful for the pen in my hand and the truth it draws blood to tell.

Grateful I survived without pretending I'm pure.

I ain't a saint.

I'm just Southern enough to remember everything,

and cold enough to finally say it...

I really hopes it get tore down, though... But hey, we family, right ...

CHAPTER 33 — STILL STANDING

I come from a place where folks smile through their teeth and call it kin.

Where hair tells the truth faster than mouths ever will.

There was a woman—lumpy in spirit, rough in temper—who carried herself like wasted horsehair left out in the rain. Had the nerve to talk about beating sense into me, like sense ever came from hands. She straightened herself, painted her face, tried to pass order off as beauty, but a mess don't stop being a mess just because it learned how to sit still.

She started with blood.

That's the part that stays coldest.

Cut roots before they could decide who they wanted to be. Snipped growth like control was love. Did it to her own babies, too. Called it care. Said it was tradition.

But we family, right?

She talked loud about my Black side, like it was a coat I put on for company. Said it when pale visitors were around, said it proud, said it false. Pretended clean while secrets stacked up behind her like unwashed dishes. Judged dirt with hands that never learned soap.

Trust turned on me once.

They called me stained for believing in somebody I shouldn't have. That's how it goes—blame sticks easier than truth. Folks will rot a whole house and point at the one cracked window.

Her mouth did more damage than any storm. Tore a bond between niece and daughter clean in half, then stood back like she didn't strike the match. Learned that behavior somewhere deep...passed down, polished, and renamed "raising."

Always commenting on my body, my strength, my shape—like measuring me kept her from shrinking. Funny how folks obsessed with holding others together are usually coming undone themselves.

Audacity lives long in the South.

Longer than shame.

I don't raise my voice.

I don't reach for revenge.

I just remember.

I remember how family gets used like a shield and a weapon depending on the day. I remember who spoke soft and cut deep. I remember how cold feels when it finally makes sense.

And when I say we family, right,

it ain't a question anymore.... I bet she will keep her motherfucking mouth close now ... barely counting money and glancing to read ...

CHAPTER 34 — SOUTHERN WOMAN

They always said, "She'll get over it...she always does."

Like pain got a clock.

Like my back was built for carrying what they refused to set down.

That's a cruel thing to say to somebody you claim you love.

But love came anyway—sideways, crooked—whether I stood as friend, blood, or enemy. Funny how fast devotion shows up after the damage is done.

Crazy thing is, they still called it family.

Disgust sat in the room with stress until my body couldn't tell the difference between them. Made me sick in a quiet way, the kind folks don't apologize for. They blamed the air, the weather, anything but themselves. Said it didn't matter. It never does—to the ones who don't pay the cost.

Regret ran loose through the house, soaked in drink and bad decisions, leaving doors open that should've stayed shut. Everybody knew. Nobody stopped it. Secrets don't stay loyal long down here—they crawl out on their own.

Once truth showed its face, I told them plain: don't speak my name with hunger, don't claim closeness you never earned. Blood don't excuse appetite. And still...we family, right?

No.

Family ain't the word.

This is a collection of choices that should've been ended early, buried deep, spared the rest of us. But here we are standing in the aftermath, pretending survival is unity.

I didn't get over it.

I got colder... and really said, "kiss all my ass and if you can't, I'll make arrangements..."

But again, we family, right ...?

CHAPTER 35 — NO APOLOGY

They say that a Black woman is worth more than any piece of jewelry or minerals ever sold...

But here I'm a Southern woman, born where the heat teaches patience and silence says more than shouting ever could.

My love life ain't never been shit, and I say that plain because dressing it up would be lying. Hope in your twenties feels like a joke they keep retelling, and somehow you still laugh like it might end different this time.

Dating felt like a dealership, a shelter, and that one friend who don't know when to leave—all mixed together. Everybody shopping. Everybody comparing. Real hearts sitting next to replicas, and the replicas always shine better under cheap lights. They called me a hopeless romantic, like it was an insult, like wanting something real was a disease you catch from believing too hard.

I never planned on being the irony. Never thought my life would be something people referenced when they wanted to feel smarter about their own bad choices. Twice—two whole times—I was almost a wife. Papers close enough to smell the ink. Futures were discussed like they were already built. And both times God heard conversations I wasn't invited to and decisions made behind my back, like I was a machine—slow, steady, doing the work while everyone else took credit.

I asked myself where my soulmate was, like it was a riddle I wasn't smart enough to solve. I wondered what I was missing while still showing up whole. I was overlooked, passed over, and treated like a quick interview because my weight made them think they already knew the answers. There was always a "next candidate." Always somebody louder, shinier, and easier to digest.

Bullshit and BBLs and bubble gum—that's what most men wanted. Something sweet with no substance. Not me. I was too smart to play dumb, too caring to let myself be disrespected, too aware to pretend love didn't come with responsibility. I wasn't built to be consumed. I was built to be known.

If I ever caused a woman tears, I've carried that. Apologized for it in my own quiet ways. Life collected its karma like it always does, and I paid my debt without arguing the total. That's why I choose carefully now. That's why I let God have His way. Because whatever ain't meant for me, He reveals—every time—no matter how put together it looks.

Sometimes I still see them. Wonder what the hype was. Notice the same patterns dressed in different clothes. That's why I hold my pillow tight at night...not lonely, just aware. Awareness can feel heavy when you're the only one carrying it.

Life of a Southern gal.

Brilliant. Beautiful. Rooted deep.

But the truth is this... most folks don't want the kind of woman who makes them grow up. They want easy. They want decoration. They want temporary.

And me?

I was never temporary.

But definitely it was always a backup plan for the needy, the homeless, and hungry...

CHAPTER 36 — NO SHRINKING

Down here, the wind don't just pass through—it remembers. It remembers names stitched into church programs, prayers folded into Sunday hats, and promises spoken soft on front porches when the cicadas got loud enough to keep secrets.

Mine been riding that wind a long time, trailing behind me through red dirt roads and narrow hallways that smelled like Pine-Sol and faith. I am a Southern woman, the kind folks misread because they don't know what to do with structure and spirit living in the same body, the kind who learned early how to sit up straight in hard pews, how to say "yes ma'am" while asking God real questions in private, the kind who wasn't raised to be loud but raised to be right.

I ain't talking about purity the way men like to reduce it, like it's something fragile or decorative—no, I mean ordained in the soul, built with intention, disciplined by God and not by fear, shaped by grandmothers who prayed over pots of greens and mamas who told you to walk proud even when your shoes were tight. Every battle I carried, I carried it through prayer, through closed doors and long nights, and through mornings where I still showed up pressed and present even when my heart was tired, and that prayer became my foundation, my weapon, and my inheritance. I didn't fight loud, didn't need an audience—I fought faithful, steady as Sunday morning, and somewhere along the way, without me even realizing it, God dressed me in a glow you can't fake and can't buy, the kind that comes from surviving what should've broken you and still choosing softness, the kind the South nods at and calls meant for more.

I remember being overlooked like it was normal, like being a Black woman with depth and discipline was something folks admired from a distance but never chose up close; remember learning how to be alone without being lonely, how to love myself in kitchens late at night, spoon tapping the pot while gospel hummed low, remember knowing I was different before I knew why, and trusting that difference anyway. I come from front-row church memories and back-row questions; from altar calls and quiet exits, from laughter that rang through family reunions and tears that fell in parked cars, and every single memory stitched me into who I am...

A woman rooted, radiant, and still becoming. If you keep reading me, you'll find a life full of grit and grace, a story that moves slow but stays with you, like Southern heat after sunset or like a prayer you didn't know you needed until it answered back.

CHAPTER 37 — FAITH WITH TEETH

I come from red dirt that stains the hem of your Sunday dress
and don't ever quite wash out.
From front porches that know more secrets than courtrooms,
from kitchens where pain simmered low and slow
right alongside the gravy.
Here comes the voodoo-spread spit,
the kind that don't come from strangers
but from folks who share your blood
and swear they love you.
That kind of magic ain't learned in books...
it's passed down with last names,
with side-eye glances,
with stories told crooked on purpose,
so by the time they reach the next year,
you don't even recognize yourself anymore.
But see, I know paperwork.
I know receipts.
And I know the weight of a pen in a steady hand.
So before anybody else decide who I am for me,
I beat them to it.
I write.

This is my lawsuit.

This is my cease-and-desist.

This is my Amen.

They say "defamation" like it's just a word,

like it don't bruise character or crack spirit,

like it don't follow you into rooms

where you ain't even said a thing yet.

Girl, boo.

You can't assassinate a soul that already survived the firing squad.

I'm suing with sentences.

Taking back my name line by line.

And baby, I don't want what you got.

I just want what's mine:

my truth,

my voice,

my peace.

They want a band-aid on their bruised egos,

want me to play nurse to wounds I didn't cause.

But I ain't your mammy.

I didn't birth your bitterness

and I sure ain't rocking it to sleep.

I'm just writing how y'all talk—

passing words like a bad game of telephone,

twisting tone, adding spice where there wasn't none,

calling it "concern" when it's really control.

So if this feel like a fair fight,

that's because it is.

Now don't get it confused,

I got grace stacked high like folded linens,

class stitched into my posture.

But if you know me,

you know I'm a Sagittarius fire-born,

arrow aimed straight,

and I don't kiss ass for warmth.

I make my own heat.

I speak my truth plain,

no sugar unless it's earned,

and yes...sometimes all hell break loose after.

That ain't because I lied.

That's because truth got a way of knocking pictures off walls

folks swore were nailed down.

Words of affirmation and informative action—

now that's how I was raised.

Say what you mean,

then show it.

They go together like gravy on anything worth eating.

And today?

It's your turn to swallow what you served.

Kiss the scar you helped make

and say it loud so the ancestors hear you.

She is the black sheep.
She is Black.
And she is proud.
I ain't an idiot.
I see the game.
I see the smirks, the whispers, the way rooms go quiet
like I don't understand the language of shade.
You think you playing in my face,
but I been studying expressions since I was knee-high.
I spent so much time with pen and paper,
trying to finally relate,
trying to make sense of why standing in my truth
felt like standing alone.
Turns out—
alone ain't empty.
It's just uncrowded.
I come from a line of women who survived being misunderstood,
misnamed, misused...
and still set the table.
Still showed up.
Still sang in church even when the choir side-eyed them.
So this is me,
lighting my own porchlight at dusk,
letting the bugs come if they must,
because I'm done dimming myself

to keep other folks comfortable in the dark.

This is my life.

My story.

My testimony.

And I will not be silenced.

CHAPTER 38 — PRAISE AFTER TEARS

A testimony carved in ice ... cold enough to make you just black
out but ...

Trauma don't always come loud.

Sometimes it shows up smiling,

calling you cousin, calling you friend,

sitting at your grandma's table

like it earned a seat.

I learned early that hurt got many faces

and some of 'em look real familiar.

Breaking away from family-friend ties

hurt worse than losing strangers... worse than a heartbreak.

'cause strangers don't know where to aim.

Jenny had four kids, three fathers,

and loyalty that packed light and traveled often.

Out of state, out-of-pocket,

out here calling chaos "goals."

I never understood why she took time

to break what I was building

with an uncle I once adored—

until the mask slipped

and the truth introduced itself.

She was connected through my grandma,

through blood-adjacent stories and borrowed trust.
Truth was, my grandma was a cover—
same way I was.
Used for access.
Used for safety.
Used till there was nothing left to drain.
She played needy real good.
Bills handled from behind bars,
money sent like clockwork,
fast food living, fast food loyalty…
your way, your rules.
I trusted you.
That was my mistake.
That chapter closed hard.
No sequel.
You asked for food,
and I slid my card without flinching,
worked through sweat and silence
to make sure your kids ate
and your precious man didn't go without.
"Oh, they don't eat this, they don't eat that"—
funny how appetite reflects upbringing.
Then you wanted me to step into foolishness,
sell poison, move dirt,
risk my freedom so you could stay comfortable.

Talking 'bout "we family,"
like family asks you to bleed for their convenience.
Crazy always cling to kindness.
That's a Southern truth.
And when I didn't bow,
didn't shrink,
didn't lay flatter…
you reached for another blade.
You lied easy.
So easy it was muscle memory.
Held one man while scouting another,
kept secrets warm and hands cleaner than truth.
You didn't want guidance.
You wanted a stepping stone.
My neck just happened to be convenient.
That's when I matched energy.
Respect left the room first
I just locked the door behind it.
You and my grandma stirred mess
then tried to call it concern,
checked me like I was the problem
knowing damn well I never named you
what your actions kept suggesting.
You chased dirty money
then clutched pearls when it followed you home.

You said things about my skin,

my mix, my lightness, my devotion of strength

as if survival ain't come in all shades.

I saw everything you did.

Time passed.

Emotions cooled.

I didn't forget…

I just stopped carrying it.

You had connections from Oxford to Saks,

state lines crossed, favors owed,

yet still cried, "family"

when accountability came knocking.

You clung to a man who stayed hungry for attention,

wore pride where discretion should've lived,

and moved reckless like truth wouldn't surface.

Wear it how you wear it.

That's your life.

This is my opinion.

And I'm done explaining it.

What cut deepest wasn't you.

It was how you used my family's hands

to hold the knife

and pressed it where I was already tender.

But hear this—

I survived the cold.

I learned which fires were real
and which ones only burned who stood too close.
I don't bleed for people
who confuse access with entitlement.
This is me walking away
without looking back,
boots steady on red clay,
heart iced over just enough
to never let that kind of hurt
take root again.
But again remind me what ... yea, we family ... Right?

CHAPTER 39 — OFFERING

Tesha was an aunt I didn't understand at first.

Didn't know how to hold her story without flinching.

Love came later...

after the world shut down

and the powder dreams and fool's gold

showed folks exactly who they were

when the lights went out.

It's heavy, playing both sides grown,

not knowing where to lay your head

or your heart.

Two lovers pulling,

three innocent souls watching,

contracts thicker than promises

'cause letting go felt like dying twice.

You carried too much.

I saw it.

I hugged you anyway.

I just wish—

Lord, I wish—you'd spoken up for me

the way I tried to shield you with silence.

Life insurance policies written in fear,

matching demons,
betting on which man might fall first,
'cause the ending already felt decided.
Ready Player One,
fighting for love
that never deserved your stamina.
You were messy sometimes...
but only when mess felt like armor.
And I get that.
Protection makes saints out of survival.
I always saw beauty in you.
Big beauty.
Even when that clown damn near burned the kitchen down,
even when smoke and mirrors filled twelve long years
that never paid you back.
You clung to an empty house,
a lonely dog,
and conditions, no woman with a crown
should ever tolerate.
You didn't deserve that.
Not then.
Not ever.
You lost weight, sure ...
but scars don't dissolve with numbers.
Your smile always told the truth, though.

That was the part nobody could steal.
You doubted yourself sometimes,
but your soul never rotted.
That matters more than people know.
The other one…
he was fast money and sweet talk,
dark and tempting like honey.
He was the bee,
and together y'all made a hive
that buzzed loud but burned quick.
I'm glad you left.
If you hadn't,
that love would've eaten you alive
and called it passion.
You'll always be my TT.
You and Tt Jerry—
the glue that holds my strength together,
the reason I know how to move through life
without folding.
So hear me now, Tesha:
never settle for a piece of a man
when you wear a whole crown.
Money, motion, and noise
won't make a stray stay.
You know the patterns.

Don't punish yourself for loving hard—
not today, not ever.
Chin up.
Chest out.
You are the one that got away,
and believe me...
that's a story he still tells.
I love you.
I want better for you.
And yeah—fuck them.
Stack your cheddar.
Choose peace.
Choose yourself.
We family, right?
So here's my prayer for you:
lavender in the air,
rolled oils warming your skin,
a soft scent pulling you back into yourself
when the world gets loud.
Your confidence keeps me afloat.
Don't ever look back
at folks who mistook your kindness for weakness
or your silence for a joke.
Texas is still there.
So is the road.

Go live.
Have at it.
This life owes you softness now
So enjoy the peace.

CHAPTER 40 — TESTIMONY

They say I talk too much, but that's just how stories get free. Down South, silence will bury you quicker than bad soil.

Time was stingy where I grew up. Folks' patience wore thinner than eye contact, and mine didn't last longer than a roach's shadow. You learned early not to look too long at nobody...because looking invited things you didn't want.

I was raised around smiles that meant harm. Men who watched like farmers sizing up land, counting seasons, waiting for what they thought they were owed. They called it joking. Called it "compliments." I learned the difference before I learned long division.

The house always smelled wrong—weed, smoke, old sweat, and something sour you couldn't scrub out. Porn books stacked like the gospel; nobody questioned. Homemade gin sloshing in jars because broken men can't afford what they crave, only what dulls it. And still, that place stayed lit, loud, and alive in all the wrong ways.

My grandmother ruled the table with a deck of cards, slapping them down like law. She won steady. Like she owned the room. Like control in one corner excused blindness everywhere else.

They said I was pretty. I wore my face hard on purpose. A shield. In my head, I named things plainly...river rats, straw teeth, and sickness you could smell before you saw it. I learned how to disappear without leaving. Sometimes that meant hiding. Sometimes that meant running to Terria's house, where quiet felt earned.

Even then, whispers followed.

"She gonna be bad when she get older."

As if a child's body was a promise instead of a warning.

Then came the rumor... I sucked dick at 11 years old ... at a park ... mean, careless, deadly. Thrown by a girl with a plastic smile and too much mouth. No proof. Just sound. Down South, that's enough to ruin a girl before she knows how to spell herself.

Bullying stuck like mildew. Sweat stains, hand-me-down clothes, and rats chewing holes through what little we had. I couldn't tell what hurt worse—being dirty, being hungry, or being told to wear it again tomorrow, like dignity was optional.

And still the men watched. Still, the family looked away. Called it love. Called it loyalty. Called it blood.

But blood don't mean protection. Sometimes it just means you learn early how to bleed quiet.

They say the South is sweet.

It is...until you taste what's underneath.

But hey, family, right...

CHAPTER 41 — SOUTHERN MEMORY

You could never ask me to choose them again...not in this life or the next. They were already dead where it mattered, rotted with half-truths and loud opinions, watching me like they knew the whole story while never touching the first real page.

Church was supposed to be a hospital. That's what they said. But all I ever saw was greed dressed in Sunday clothes, sickness calling itself salvation. Regular mornings, before the sun even stretched good, my sisters and I would wake up to the first sound of the day...

Shut the fuck up!!!! Damn already ...

Just like that. Dawn hadn't even finished cracking, and God already got cursed out. I remember thinking, "Well damn... what happens now?" Like lightning was supposed to strike the linoleum.

My grandmother would clutch her Bible tight, knuckles white, foot tapping like she was fixing to sprint from judgment. Something stayed heavy on her mind, and I was just a kid trying to read a room full of adults who refused to read themselves.

I'm grown now, but chaos don't forget you. It took so much from me, then had the nerve to wonder why my attitude shows up loud at funerals...why grief sits sharp on my shoulders instead of soft. Folks say the pastor spoke truth, and maybe he did, but truth don't land when the devil makes a scene just to remind everybody he still got keys to the building.

My grandmother's boyfriend cursed God like it was his full-time job. Wore anger on his face so long it set permanent. At night, he'd holler in his sleep, spirits tearing at him the same way he tore into us—words sharp, mean, careless. Yelling that he wasn't loved. Cursing the kids. Demanding what he thought he deserved.

Then he'd drink himself stupid, fall out hard, ambulance lights flashing like a warning nobody wanted to read. Folks asking if he was dead this time. Nah. Hard head. Stubborn to the bone. Some people survive out of spite alone.

And there we were...still growing, still watching, still learning what not to become.

Some things should've been dragged straight to the altar and handled right there, but down South, we call it "family" and sit in it instead. We don't comment. We listen. We swallow it whole.

That's embarrassment in its finest form... like damn...polished, prayed over, and passed down like tradition.

And me?

I remembered everything.... If you only knew you wouldn't have even stayed that long at all ...

But yet it was very common ...

CHAPTER 42 — QUIET VICTORY

Before it got this bad, I cared.

That's the part folks don't believe, but it's the truest thing about me.

Back then, God had a veil over my eyes...

thin like church lace, soft enough to let light in but strong enough to blur the lies.

I forgave dry lips that never meant what they said.

Forgave stories that didn't add up.

Kept calling it love. Kept calling it faith.

Southern folks good at that.

We endure.

We pray.

We hush our own knowing.

It took me carrying my grandmother to safety, hands steady, heart racing...

just to turn around and finally see the whole house burning.

Not smoke.

Fire.

And when it hit me, it hit hard.

I cried like I died.

Like something holy was torn straight out my body.

I bled with two unborn futures that never got to breathe Southern air,

never got names whispered over them.
That pain don't leave...
it just learns how to sit quiet.

Still, I kept going.
Because that's what we do down here.
We bury things and wake up early anyway.
Cousins saved me some nights.
Kitchen-table talks.
Low voices.
Truth passed like a bottle.
But family...
Family don't care till it's their blood on the floor.
Then come the tears...
loud, messy, too damn late.
I danced around that decision day and night.
Didn't post out of spite.
Posted because silence is how evil gets comfortable.
Because people scared to look straight at what's real
And Lord...
watching voodoo get conjured right in front of me...
pieces of my hair kept like trophies,
pictures of me living on phones I never held,
all because somebody's ego couldn't survive the truth?
That'll shake a soul.

Cameras watching.

Flashes popping.

And just like that...

2025 passed like a bad dream you can't wake from.

Everything faded so fast, I had to ask God if this was real

or just another test dressed up as a lifetime.

I kept dancing.

Dancing through sour patches of freedom.

how y'all not in jail still don't make sense to me.

Guess smooth talking and shaking the right hands paid off.

Dirty river money always finds a way downstream.

But it's still dirty.

Still soaked.

Still running through veins that share hate like it's genetic.

This ain't math, but it's numbers all the same.

This ain't fiction, but it plays like a movie...

and I'm watching it in full 3D, no escape.

Some nights I whisper,

God, please save me.

Not from death but from

from understanding too much.

I don't get it.

But I know this:

I'm still here.

And God don't drag nobody this far just to drop them in the dark.

So I trust.

Even tired.

Even bruised.

Even knowing the South can be beautiful and cruel in the same breath.

The big deal ain't what they did.

The big deal is I survived seeing it.

And that...

that's the truth; God don't waste.

Because eyes are the key to the soul, and mine has definitely seen a lot; I guess that's why God gave me foresight.

CHAPTER 43 — STILL WALKING

Thank you, Barbie ...

Down South, folks learn early that blood don't always mean belonging. Sometimes it just mean proximity to chaos.

I had a cousin by marriage like that—one of those women who needed eyes on her the way fire needs air. Heels higher than her sense, weave matted together like secrets nobody ever washed clean. A hard face, sharp as a man's jaw, but a body always thin or breaking—never settled. We called her Cavity, 'cause she rotted whatever she bit into.

Cavity was wild before I ever learned how to spell my own name. Pregnant at fourteen, loud as sin, rebelling just to hear herself echo. Always in somebody's face, daring them to look away. She thought that made her a star. Down here, we just call that trouble with good lighting.

Abortions followed her like ghosts she refused to name, and old men followed her like a bad smell...because she let them. She only came around to drop off her replicas when she needed a fix, hands shaking but pride still loud. Coconut powder stayed perfect though...she made sure of that. Appearances mattered more than souls ever did to her.

She clung to our uncle like a bad habit nobody questioned out loud. After that, things started moving fast, the way disasters do when nobody steps in. She looked like a Barbie—clean, hood, and misunderstood if you asked her...but Jails knew her government name. Men knew her sweetness. That's where the nickname really came from: she was a craving, not a meal.

Fierce, reckless, and empty. A whole shitshow wrapped in confidence. Truth be told, she wore thickness better than bones.

Coke carved her down to something sharp and broken, and she never put the pieces back. Multiple abortions, still no main ones raised right…kids always "under construction," even when they grown enough to know better. Animal cruelty, too. A moment so foul it stained everything that came after. A fucked-up mother doing fucked-up things, like the South ain't seen that pattern before.

So tell me why I had to be related to you, even by marriage. Undercover chaos with a familiar last name.

I remember Nicki Minaj blasting out of a bright red Impala, bass rattling windows and nerves. When she wasn't around, she was making some man holler… dancing for money, for power, for whatever the song told her she was worth that night. Still sleeping with her baby daddy while he sold drugs like he sold promises, only visible in the dark.

She was spoiled and loud about it. Flaunted every blessing like it couldn't be revoked. And maybe that's why she finally snapped…beat the one who birthed her to death and then left her to rot, like love never stood a chance. The South knows how to keep secrets, but it also knows how to keep score.

She still in my prayers. Not because she was right… But because darkness don't scare God, and mercy ain't mine to ration. She gone now. Time will finish the story the way it always does.

Cold earth. Quiet road.

Battle already decided.

Anyway, cavity check…

CHAPTER 44 — CALLING

Now I know my readers are sniffin' around like hounds on a hot trail, tails up, noses working overtime. "Get to it," you say. Belt to ass. I hear you. Love y'all, though, but who am I? Or better yet... who is she?

The audacity of even askin'.

If I had to name myself, I'd say Lil Southern Belle, with limits folks love to underestimate. See, I'm young, but wisdom done settled in my bones early. I was kissed by honeysuckles and corrected by stick-to-your-spine truths. I ain't a drink you sip polite—I'm a limited edition pour, slow burn, no refills.

They'll call me chubby. I'll call it perfectly curved, thank you kindly. But that still ain't the word. My mind? Baby, that's a forbidden library...knowledge stacked on shelves nobody was supposed to reach. Being a gifted child of God come with a price, and I been payin' interest with grace.

I used to be a firecracker—short fuse, loud joy—but time smoothed me out, didn't dull me. I'm a silly chick, a real-life joker, the kind that don't perform at you but pulls up a chair and makes you feel at home. My voice carry hymns—strength braided with passion and a little charm I never asked for. God just went ahead and did His big one.

I'm short, pretty, and piglet-nosed just right—not wide and not shy. My lips always get there first 'cause folks be tryin' to figure me out like I'm Maybelline. I don't need makeup—ain't flexin', just testifyin'. I come from a line of beautiful women. That's God's little test to men: beauty, brains, and a glass of sweet iced tea served buckled tight. Saddle up.

I like stayin' home. Keeps me safe from energy vampires—folk who wanna steal your glow and call it fate. Don't get it twisted, though. I'm the life of the party. I don't need an introduction; the room notices. Good, bad, sideways—oh well. Sagittarius can't be tamed. We free spirits. Love us, talk with us—that's how you get your money's worth.

If I could change one thing, it'd be the chances I gave. But I won't argue with God's pen. He already wrote it. So what do I do? Easy. I write.

Tucked in bed, feet rubbed raw from the day, hot cocoa in hand, phone warm, words pourin' like motivation. And baby, if you readin' this...Yeah, you consider yourself my sweetest sugarcane, with a splash of lemon and a slow sip.

Most important thing? I ain't no coward. I'm reserved. I don't bite back at folks poor in spirit but rich in opinions. I just let 'em taste their own tea.

All this comin' from me... Girl, yeah. Gotta keep you on your toes. Bein' an author ain't light work...

But you already knew that, didn't you?

But hey, again, we family ... What y'all say, howdy, right?

CHAPTER 45 — DAUGHTER FREED

Some people are just like grit under the fingernail...

Now if I'm bein' clear—real clear—options and opinions walk hand in hand like sisters wearin' their daddy's last name. Folks love to mix 'em up and call it truth. Anyhow...

I had a pa who wasn't blood but might as well been stitched in. Fit like a glove that warmed you right—just not right in the mind. Eyes sour as spoiled milk, always squintin' like the world owed him somethin'. I called him Pop-Pop Douglas, and Lord... that man was a certified fool. Always hollerin' "stand down," like life was a war zone and we was recruits.

"You must think I'm crazy," he'd bark, "or all that yin-yang you talkin'—bullshit."

But my favorite saying of his—burned into my memory like a brand—was

"You must think you slicker than owl shit."

Meaning nothin' got past him. Or so he thought.

Truth is, crazy don't always know it's crazy. Pop Pop walked around like a mad dog on a short chain—cigarette glued to his mouth, gun closer than his own damn shadow. Rifle was his best friend. Mean as a junkyard dog guarding nothin' but bitterness. Just a bunch of boondock alcoholics playin' house with hell.

And yet he loved my grandma.

Loved her in that crooked, toxic way that keeps folks stuck. Big age gap, big imbalance, but she was his shelter, his excuse, his "all in one." So he never left. Couldn't. Stuck like flies on shit. Lord knows why that mix ever came together, but love be crazy like that, especially when it don't know when to let go.

He always wore that hard face. Watched from afar. When he was sober—rare but real—he was steady. A retired veteran by his own account. "I been shot and stabbed—you don't know nothin' 'bout pain."

But I did.

Pain sounded like yellin'.

Pain looked like pullin' weapons 'cause my grandma dared think about leavin'.

Pain was cursin' her out in public and lovin' her quiet in private...then expectin' loyalty like fear was romance. And still... she held on. Held on like underwear already ridin' too deep to fix without makin' it worse.

That was Pop Pop Douglas.

An embarrassment wrapped in a warning label.

Cussin' God every Sunday on holy ground.

Sometimes I'd sit there thinkin', "Lord, strike lightning right now." 'Cause how you swish poison in your mouth and speak on God like He ain't listenin'? But that's patience for you... God's patience, not ours. He sees it all. That's why I just stood tall. Quiet. Watchful. Learning what not to become.

So yeah—stand your ground and buckle up.

Welcome to the nut house.

Where survival teaches you discernment,

and stories grow teeth.

CHAPTER 46 — BLOOD NO LONGER BINDS

Coming in with no filter ...

Every project in a Black neighborhood got a story, but not the kind they whisper when they bad-mouth Glenaddie or Constantine Homes' projects like it's a sport.

"Don't go over there."

"They bad."

"They shootin'."

Like danger, don't know how to creep quiet. Like it don't tiptoe at night and pick the innocent 'cause they tired, broke, or just mindin' their own damn business.

Females—ain't sayin' names 'cause the names know who they are—switch baby daddies faster than pacifiers hit the floor. Tragic... or just a new magic trick. Depends who you ask. Ask the hood men in interviews or just lean against a car long enough and they'll tell you the same recycled line:

"All they wanna do is get fucked."

But most of y'all ain't like your granddaddies who paid bills, fixed leaks, and didn't need applause for doin' the bare minimum. I ain't innocent—I live here too—but "monkey see, monkey do" ain't never built nothin' but circles.

What always puzzled me is how folks watch my body like it's cable TV. Eyes countin' what I can pull, what I ride in, what I wear, and who I talk to. Ponderin' eyes, sharp tongues.

"We family, right?"

Yeah—family with receipts and resentment.

"Fat bitch."

As if that's new.

Baby, I tug, I roll, I exist. I call myself protein to a malnourished ego and keep it pushin'. Don't be mad 'cause you gotta step your game up and all you got is borrowed personality and recycled confidence.

The neighbors? Lord, argue over air.

Who said what?

Who looked wrong?

Over some dude who either gay, confused, or just a loan you borrowin' 'til your baby daddy get out of jail. Temporary men, permanent drama.

Perks and Hennessy breath hangin' in the heat. Mouths talkin' loud while swallowin' karma whole. Stamps burned out. Bodies paid for with surgery money and regret.

"You done, honey?"

Never. They never done.

Baddies on Zeus ain't got shit on Alabama. I promise you. Too much raw, unfiltered, uncut talent down here—most of it hid behind fronts so hard they forgot who they were before survival became a costume.

"We family," they say.

Nah. More like Hennessy and hell—mixed heavy and served warm.

Survivin' y'all feel like a video game set on expert mode. No cheats. No save point. And yeah... sometimes I fail.

But I keep playin'.

Cold.

Laughin'.

Southern as hell but ducked behind walls that has plenty of stories to tell.

But again, we family, right? It's all a game, but pride wears a mask that is definitely shame.

CHAPTER 47 — THIS IS REAL

My, my, what a man would do for a wet set of four pairs of lips ... You crazy aint cha ... Yep, I know an unknown call but here we go ...

Down here, folks swear they've seen everything, but let a Black woman stand ten toes down in herself and the whole county start actin' unfamiliar. They been sexualizin' us since forever—turnin' confidence into invitation and peace into temptation. Still... even I wasn't ready for that mail.

Picture this: hot Southern sun, screen door creakin', and the mailman handin' me an envelope like it carried a family secret. Alabama divorce papers. Addressed to me. Official. Stamped. Serious. Only problem? I ain't never been nobody's wife.

I had to lean on the doorframe and laugh. One of them laughs that come from deep in your chest. Because baby... It's just pussy. Do it really run ya world like this? Got a grown man losin' his bearings, signin' papers, imaginin' vows that never happened?

Now don't get me wrong—power comes in many forms down South. Some folks got land. Some got money. Some got a last name heavy enough to bend spines. But every now and then, there's a woman who don't have to touch a thing to cause damage. Just her absence alone will scramble a man's senses clean loose.

UPS said they couldn't trace it. No sender. No return address. Just confusion sealed in an envelope. And honestly? I smiled.

Whoever sent it, I just wanna say thank you—because that was the best backhanded top-tier compliment I ever received. Divorced without ever bein' married? Lord, that's talent. I don't even know if I turned you down or simply didn't notice you the first time... but this? This feel like a second attempt to reach me.

Hi—we family, right?

Are you my baby daddy... or just a scrub I kicked to the side and forgot about? Either way, much Honey Bunches of Oats, because whatever the idea of me did to you clearly had you wantin' to toast.

So cheers, baby.

And muah.

I folded that paper nice and neat and kept on livin', because I don't answer to imaginary husbands, anonymous admirers, or men bold enough to file paperwork but too shy to sign their name. Down here, we say if it ain't yours, don't claim it.

And if a woman got you divorcin' ghosts?

That ain't love.

That ain't lust.

That's just her bein' unforgettable.

But hey, I can't help that I'm irresistible... But divorce papers , though? What's next ...?

CHAPTER 48 — THE CHAIN STOPPED HERE

Down here on Southern soil, where the dirt remembers blood and prayer the same way, my life didn't come gentle. It came swinging. Fuck shit. Weird shit. Straight bullshit. Not dramatic — just relentless. And still, I stood long enough to see it clearly: I am not who I used to be, and I am not broken for surviving it.

I am okay. Chosen folk always are — even when the battle is brutal.

God don't pick the weak for hard assignments. He hands them early to the strong and watches them grow muscle in places pain tried to hollow out. My wings don't need feathers to work. My courage was baked into my bones before I ever knew fear. This story didn't come from survival—it came from authority.

And it ends with me.

No more curses dragged behind us like chains. No more trauma passed down like family tradition. I paid enough tears to flood generations, and now the world gon' hear what it cost. Still upright. Still breathing. Still graceful while the fire runs through me. That's my hallelujah—not pretty, but powerful.

The Holy Spirit didn't visit me. It moved in. Burned off the lies, the fear, the pretending. You don't know how good God is until you realize. He trusted you to be the strongest soldier in your bloodline—young, alone, and still obedient. Spiritual warfare ain't loud; it's quiet victories while tears hit the floor and chains shatter behind you.

I did this for my mama.

I did this for my sister.

I did this for every voice that was silenced before it learned how to scream.

I snapped the camel's back and told the truth anyway. Yes, I went through hell, and God's hand never left my shoulder. No bullet, no paperwork, no spell, and no blood sacrifice meant to break me ever had permission. "Touch not my anointed" ain't scripture on a page ... It's a warning stamped on my life.

Blessed beyond measure.

Still standing.

Still dangerous to darkness.

When I'm done, people will be free. Not entertained ... free. Speak up. The world needs to hear it raw. We are family, but fear don't live here no more.

I am exactly who God created me to be. A mouthpiece. A breaker of cycles. A motivator for the weary and the wounded. And don't get it twisted—this ain't just a story.

This is my offering.

Heavy. Holy.

Laid down on Southern soil.

I'm always covered by his glory so I give my praises to the most high ... holy, holy , may he reign forever and ever all over my soul ... When my time comes, I go with honor and gladness because I'm going home to see that pretty lady that missed all my years ... my creator , my father ... basically, my everything.

CHAPTER 49 — CHAOS AFTER DARK

Imagine bein' here where the walls don't just hold sound ...they memorize it.

You hear everything. Every lie rehearsed. Every threat recycled. Every mouth that won't rest even when the world asleep.

Three in the mornin', Lord.

That's when the noise get bold.

Some fool hollerin' like volume equals victory, yellin' useless battle cries to nobody but the dark. Ain't no point, ain't no plan—just noise lookin' for witnesses. Projects got a way of auctionin' space to hell's loudest bidders. Always somebody auditionin' for chaos, always somebody convinced the block need to hear their inner mess.

Hell on wheels—that's what I call 'em.

Shooters in spirit if not in flesh. Words sharp enough to pierce sleep, bullets in their mouth, whether they ever pull a trigger or not. Danger don't always run—sometimes it just talks too damn much.

I sit quiet.

Still as red clay after rain.

Listenin' like I'm waitin' on somethin' ancient to hum back—some old warning, some inherited instinct that tell you when to stay, when to move, when to pray without sayin' a word.

Crazy world we livin' in.

Mega microphones attached to folks with nothin' sacred to say. A mix of ego, insecurity, and infection—loud, irritated, and placed where it don't belong. Why disturb sleep like it owe you somethin'? Why drag everybody into a fight that ain't even real?

But we family, right?

That's what they say when accountability don't live there.

So I talk to God instead. Ask Him to get me outta this hole. Not bitter. Not broken. Just intact. Ask Him to lift me clean, to reverse what keeps circlin' these buildings like a curse that don't know when to quit.

I don't match the noise.

I don't answer it.

I outlast it.

Because down here, survival ain't loud.

It's quiet.

Cold.

Watchful.

And God don't miss His daughters...especially the ones He taught how to stay still while hell shows its whole hand...

CHAPTER 50 — WATCHED BUT UNMOVED

Ain't got no tea on me—this ho think she TMZ.

Down here, folks mistake proximity for access and gossip for insight. They swear they know you 'cause they watched you bleed once, like pain make you public property.

Imagine bein' me, where people try to weaponize the very wounds I laid down as an offering. Not for sympathy. Not for applause. But 'cause some folks needed to know survivin' was possible without losin' your mind. They thought that meant I was easy. Thought grace meant soft. Thought oil on my head meant I wouldn't strike back.

Girl... play it safe and find somethin' to do.

They hunt my name like I'm a lottery ticket, scratchin' at rumors, hopin' today the prize fall out. Still ain't won. Not yet. And the wild part? Your biggest critics always end up your biggest fans—studying you harder than scripture, memorizing movements they'll never live up to.

I'm short in the flesh but tall where it count.

Spiritually ranked.

And it rumbles.

That kind of pressure don't need a microphone. It shake rooms without ever openin' its mouth. It's the kind of awakening that sit behind the teeth, feelin' like a shout but holdin' still outta respect for the ones who bled before I ever took a breath. Restraint ain't weakness ...it's inheritance.

You can't hurt me.

Not after how I lived.

What you got ain't a weapon; it's your foot lodged deep in your own ass, and now you mad 'cause it hurt.

Folks gon' keep stickin' their nose where it don't belong. Down South, curiosity come dressed as concern. But couldn't be me. Never was.

We family, right?

That phrase be a chant. A burden. A threat dressed like loyalty.

Three words carry destruction down here—not "I love you," but "we family," right? It excuse foolishness, protect harm, and demand silence all at once. And I see it for what it is.

Imagine bein' me—stomachin' pain without spillin' tears, hearin' God whisper, Wait, my child. I'm close. I'm near. So I wait. Not empty. Not alone. Covered in prayers, I can feel brush past my skin like warm air before a storm.

And then I hear it clear as church bells in cold wind:

Lena, my love, you the one to break the fuse.

Now watch how the devil cut loose when the circuit don't work no more.

Spiritual warfare ain't dramatic—it's constant.

Mind.

Heart.

Spirit.

And still... I'm here.

Southern.

Cold.

Standing.

And that's the part they never know what to do with.

But again, we family, right? Nah, it's just hidden resentment mixed with a shot of spite ...

155

CHAPTER 51 — FAMILIAR ROT

Imagine being me.

I know folks talking now 'cause the anger they been sittin' in finally leaked through the floorboards. Funny how it was cool when they did it—whispered, plotted, and dirtied my name like it was communal property—but when I open my mouth, suddenly I'm the problem.

Girl, please.

I chew gum and watch. That's my talent. Learned early how underground possums move—quiet, sideways, always hungry, always claimin' family when it's convenient. And every time I hear that word—family—my stomach turn. Yuck. What a lie folks use to stay unaccountable.

This house got history. Not the kind you frame—spiritual residue soaked into the walls. Evil don't knock here; it already got a key. Folks drawn to it like flies to heat, braggin' loud about "doing good" while parking shiny cars in front of rot. Streets and treats talk big, but the soul be bankrupt. Braggin' on sin like it's success. Lord, bless whoever cross paths with Uncle Unknown, 'cause he don't lead—he drags.

I've seen warnings come before destruction every time. They come dressed as weddings, smiles, and sunlight. Parades before collapse. Folks think cheating free 'cause it don't cost money—but it costs towns, families, bodies, and futures. Everything spread when nobody wash their hands of truth.

Uncle Unknown, barely standin'. Pride keepin' him upright more than bones. Always needin' attention, mistakin' noise for relevance. I don't know how people get comfortable livin' with decay—rats in the corners, snakes in the walls, and chaos treated like decor. But when you raised in clutter, peace feel suspicious.

Short men with tall egos. Sticky situations nobody admit to. Theft dressed up as survival. Manners never learned 'cause invitations never came. And me? I stand there wonderin' how blood stretch this thin. How we share a name but not a nature.

They call me crazy 'cause I see it.

But this ain't madness—this is eyesight.

This my life. A reality show nobody asked for. Soulless spirits walkin' around like they own the place, playin' holy with simple prayers and loud mouths. And I'm done pretendin' it don't stink just 'cause it's familiar.

I had enough.

Let it crumble.

Some things deserve to fall so the ground can finally breathe again.

Southern.

Cold.

And tellin' the truth anyway...

CHAPTER 52 — NOTHING CLEAN ENTERED

Imagine being a side piece for two whole years and still not realizing the smell you carry ain't just the house—it's you. That kind of blindness takes commitment. Brave, even. Brave enough to laugh through another woman's pain while never once meeting a bar of soap halfway.

You sat comfortable in filth, giggling like decay was cute, while my grandmother was still breathing air you poisoned with your presence. That takes a special kind of trifling. The kind Bernie Mac would've side-eyed and called exactly what it was.

Uncle Unknown never had standards—just appetite. He reached for anything except the truth. And you came carrying sickness of the spirit, dragging mess through a house that didn't invite you. Everything you touched soured. Everything you laughed through rotted faster.

Bare bones wrapped in noise. Loud, with nothing to offer but heat and damage. No repairs, no contribution—just infestation energy. Parasites thrive where accountability don't live. That's a Southern fact.

And every time the truth knocked, y'all played the same song:

"She lyin'. She lyin'."

On repeat.

Like denial was a contract you signed in blood.

Robbed peace. Robbed dignity. Then hid behind confusion like it was innocence. Ain't nothing spiritual about disease—

physical or otherwise. Some things don't need prayer; they need removal.

But of course...

We family, right?

That word always show up when responsibility leaves. No ownership. No repentance. Just a house run like a backroom, morals rented by the hour, minds still chained to whatever taught them survival without self-respect.

Southern soil sees it all.

Filth don't stay hidden forever.

And silence don't mean ignorance—it means judgment is waiting.

Cold truth?

I outgrew the room.

Y'all just stayed in the mess and called it loyalty.

And that's the end of it.

CHAPTER 53 — PERMANENT STAINS

Down here, surprises don't jump out from behind doors—they sit on the couch, legs crossed, acting confused. Uncle Unknown. Junior. And Aunt Mrs. Hamburger with a slice of cheese on top. All of them standing in pure disbelief, like they don't know just how crossed they are by the very stains they been dragging through life.

And baby, some stains ain't funny.

They permanent.

That kind you can't scrub out with bleach, prayer, or denial. The kind that cling to you like ticks—feeding, bloated, convinced they belong. Gotta whistle at 'em, snap fingers, and talk slow, 'cause obedience is the only language they halfway understand. Even then? They still don't listen.

Trifling.

Trifling again.

Trifling in cursive.

Whole sacks of shit and slugs calling me brainwashed or crazy , like courts don't keep records and phones don't remember numbers. As if paper don't talk louder than lies when it's time. Lord, the way demons dance in daylight now—no shame, no cover, just bold and barefoot in the truth.

Sometimes I think if I had holy water in my hand, I'd have baptized the whole scene just to watch what scattered.

They move like cramped creatures in sewer pipes—grown bodies, small thinking, surviving off recycled waste and calling it family structure. What kinfolk will do to keep broken leverage is something else. They'll twist truth, slap a label on it, and then call you crazy for naming exactly what you see.

Peacocks got more sense. At least they know when to fan out and when to shut up.

But down here?

They breathe like constipation—stuck, strained, and waiting on relief that never comes. Always anticipating a payout, a benefit, or a moment where somebody else finally spills so they don't have to. Been crying over sour buttermilk so long they forgot what fresh looks like.

And still—

We family, right?

That word always show up when accountability leaves the room. Used like duct tape over a cracked foundation. Loud. Sticky. Useless.

So I stand where I always been:

Observing, unbothered, clocked in to truth.

Lit when I need to be.

Silent when it cuts deeper.

Because being Southern ain't about sweetness.

It's about knowing exactly who crossed you—

and letting God handle the rest.

Child.... A big hot ass mess, but of course from the best with these negros.

CHAPTER 54 — HEAVEN WHISPERED

Testimony without begging to be believed....

People might read my story and shed a tear or two, but most won't realize the kind of strength it takes to still be standing after telling it. They'll skim past the backbone it cost me to finally break open, not knowing that testimony don't come from comfort—it comes from pressure.

Some folks call me crazy.

I call myself strong.

Because God and I know exactly what's going on.

Most mornings I sit still, real still, before the world get loud. The sun barely up, air heavy with dew, and heaven whispering like it always does when you finally learn how to listen. I hear prayers that ain't spoken out loud. Feel the Holy Spirit activating—mind, body, and spirit—moving through me like a system check from glory itself.

Tears come, but they don't feel weak. They feel clean. Like confirmation.

I'm poised right where I'm supposed to be. Strong. Standing tall. Rooted like a Southern landscape that's seen storms but never forgot how to bloom.

Now let me tell you what the Holy Spirit feel like—because it ain't quiet and it ain't timid.

It feel like fire wrapped in cold air. A fierce heat mixed with comfort. Love with authority. It dance through you like you just woke up to your spiritual rhythm and your feet don't even belong to you no more. It make you wanna jump up and shout, but sometimes you gotta calm yourself down and whisper "hallelujah" under your breath so the praise don't spill too fast.

Shackles shake loose without permission. Glory overflow like it's been waitin' on you to catch up.

I feel angels I can't see—hands steadying me, grip firm, gentle but unmovable. There's a flame inside me that don't burn out, just burns right. Dancing like it ain't nobody's business. Sweet as cold water on a hot Southern day—refreshing, necessary, life-saving.

I swear, folks don't know how good God is. How consistent. How intentional. How near.

But I do.

And that's enough for me.

The song that play while I write this give me goosebumps every time, like heaven hummin' along just to remind me I'm not alone. This story—this testimony—ain't just words. It's my lifeline. My blood. My voice.

And I will never back down from it.

Glory. Hallelujah.

Found and proud it takes courage ...

CHAPTER 55 — GOD IS MY ALIBI

Im sacred but perfectly imperfect in gods design but as i call a beautiful puzzle piece ...

Sometimes the memories hit me all at once—

Like life hit rewind and pressed play without askin'. I've watched myself die once in the physical and twice in the spirit and still come back reborn. Came back a magnolia-brown-sugar babe, soft and dangerous in the same breath.

My eyes always been the key to my soul. Folks stare like they're lookin' for answers they ain't ready to hold. I used to wonder how and why—but I don't no more. God is my alibi.

The tears people don't see?

They heavier than life itself. Every one of 'em carry memory. Weight. Receipt. Some call it pain. I call it evidence. Karma don't always come loud—sometimes it come as the Lord sittin' back, lettin' time testify.

I watch now. Quiet. Still.

Life keep movin' while God clear rooms like an angel walkin' pavement. Big sweep comin'. Dust don't argue when judgment pass through. This ain't revenge—this is alignment.

This is my war cry, and I don't have to raise my voice.

I let God handle what I can't see, hear, or trace through calls, conversations, paperwork, or fake friends with holy mouths and dirty intentions. I'm sittin' still while He work. Sprinkled. Covered. Anointed. Armored.

Do you know how powerful it is not to move and still win?

You ain't seen nothin' yet.

My God is awesome. He move mountains without makin' announcements. He do things eyes ain't witnessed yet, and still folks get mad at my testimony—like survival is offensive when it don't include them.

I see demons. I smell their hatred. And baby, it stink next to my light.

People read and cry and ask how I lived through it.

Simple.

Nothing but God.

He don't miss. Ever.

And when He show up? It's chef's kiss over my favor—sealed in salvation, grafted through grace, and signed in blood by His only Son.

That's how I'm still here.

That's how I stay standing.

That's how I kept going ...

CHAPTER 56 — THE PEN INSTEAD OF FIRE

She say this and that, run her mouth like a screen door in a storm—but I'm still writin'.

Because truth be told, I got every reason to crash out. Plenty.

But I choose the pen instead of the fire, 'cause writin' lets the pressure breathe. It loosen the knots folk never knew was tied in me.

There were times—more than folks would guess—where I didn't know what happy felt like. I lived, cracked open. Forever bent. But not broken enough to numb myself with drugs or disappear into smoke. My fight was quieter than that.

My mind and my heart been playin' tug-of-war since I was young. I finally let my heart win. And when it did, I accepted a hard truth: people gon' do what they do. So I stayed. I answered calls that only came to set me up. I watched folks smile in my face, then laugh later while braggin' on somebody else's hard work like it was their own.

Yeah—you the man for now.

But time got a way of exposin' borrowed shine.

I seen folks brag on stepkids while still married to mess. Still broke down. Still refusin' to divorce lies from truth. I never understood why folks dance so hard around honesty when it's easier to tango straight with the truth. Just say it.

Just say, "We did her wrong."

She didn't deserve that.

My niece.

My granddaughter.

Whatever name feel safest to hide behind.

But I know how y'all operate. Accountability don't live where ego rent-free. Same way those fake tears fell when it was your sister. Your daughter. The woman who birthed me. Tears ain't repentance when they dry too fast.

After everything I did for you, I'm worth a speck?

A dust crumb in your vision?

Honestly, I ain't surprised. Disappointment get familiar when blood forget it owe you decency.

But hear me clear—if there is another life after this one, think long on the karmic debt you stackin'. If it don't come now, it'll come later. Interest included. Time always collect.

And still... after everything?

After the love, the labor, and the loyalty?

Y'all still say, we family, like it's a shield instead of a sentence.

So I keep writin'.

Not to crash out.

Not to beg.

But to remember who I was, who I am, and who I refused to become.

Because down South, we learn early:

Sometimes survivin' your own people is the hardest testimony you'll ever tell.

And I'm still here to tell it.

CHAPTER 57 — EVERYBODY TOUGH UNTIL TRUTH BREATHES

Pay less flip-flops ...

I came up where the heat teaches lessons before people do. Where hit dogs scream all summer like they're keeping score, and grown folks smile while handing you burdens you didn't ask for. My life didn't start with lullabies—it started with listening. Listening for footsteps, for tone changes, for danger dressed up as family.

Down South, they'll call it love while asking you to bleed quiet. They'll say we family, like that's a holy shield, like blood alone can forgive neglect, betrayal, or harm. I learned early that blood don't mean brave—it means silent. And silence was the first thing they tried to teach me.

I was the one expected to hold it together. To show up. To fix. To cover. To make miracles out of thin money and thin air. I handled problems that weren't mine and carried weights grown folks dropped on purpose. I stayed present, answered calls, and gave grace where it wasn't earned. They mistook my strength for consent.

Truth is, I watched small things expose big lies. Twenty-five dollar flip-flops opened doors that had been locked for years. Money slid wrong. Stories changed shape. Folks got loud when they thought nobody was listening, then real quiet when witnesses showed up. Guilt has a way of rattling a house even when nobody says its name.

They talked on me. They talked about my child. That's when the ground shifted. Down here, you can disrespect a woman and still expect her to pray—but bring her baby into your mess, and the South loses its manners real fast. Porches turn into courtrooms. Smiles fall off faces. And the truth gets loud enough to carry.

Funny thing about noise—it don't last. The loudest ones always go silent when the air clears. Blame starts moving like it's trying to find a new home. Everybody tough until the story breathes. Everybody righteous until accountability knocks.

They tried to hand me that old line again—we family, right?

Family that throws knives with one hand and hugs with the other. Family that funds curses and calls it duty. Family that lets outsiders run the house because control feels easier than truth.

Nah. I don't deal with cursed spirits. I don't rewrite my memories to make other people comfortable. And I don't owe silence to folks who needed me quiet to stay clean.

I learned how to count every dollar and still make it stretch. Learned how to warm a home when nobody taught me how. Learned survival before comfort, honesty before peace. You can't intimidate someone who already rebuilt herself without help. You can't outsmart someone who had to learn life the hard way and kept the receipts.

So let them yell. Let them rewrite. Let guilt wear them down in the quiet—it always does. I'll be busy living free, telling the truth plain, and cutting ties so clean it scares anybody who benefited from my silence.

Down South, when a woman finally speaks,

the whole house feels it.

And when she keeps walking after?

That's the part they'll never forgive.

CHAPTER 58 — PREPARED, NOT PERFECT

A love letter wrapped in my prayers that I bear and patience that is dearly ...

Dear God,

I'm talking to You about him again.

My future husband.

The man You're already holding for me.

I don't know his name yet, but You do.

You know the sound of his laugh,

the weight of his hands,

the way his heart beats when he's tired but still faithful.

So Lord, when You check on him tonight,

tell him he's being prayed for, real soft, down South.

I ask You to cover him, Father.

Heal what he don't talk about.

Ease the places where life pressed too hard.

Teach him love that ain't loud but steady—

the kind that shows up and stays.

Lord, I'm not asking for perfect.

I'm asking for prepared.

A man who fears You more than he fears losing me.

A man who leads with prayer and listens with patience.

A king who knows his crown came from You.

I've waited, God.
Not just sitting still, but growing.
Learning how to love without losing myself.
Learning how to rest without giving up.
If I've ever rushed before, forgive me—
I understand now that good things take time.
When he comes, Lord,
let him find me whole.
Let him find me kind.
Let him find me ready to honor him,
not because I am small,
but because love rooted in You feels safe.
I imagine him sometimes, God.
Strong but gentle.
Careful with his words.
Eyes deep like a southern sky after rain—
the kind you can trust won't change on you overnight.
You saw every tear I cried in loneliness.
Every almost-love that didn't choose me right.
You heard me when I said I'd rather wait than settle.
Thank You for protecting my heart when I didn't know how.
So until the day You place his hand in mine,
keep working on us.

Keep aligning our steps.
Keep our hearts soft and our faith strong.
And when he finally walks into my life,
I'll know it was You—
not coincidence, not chance—
but answered prayer.
With patience, hope, and love,
Your daughter

CHAPTER 59 — TOO AWAKE

Down South, folks will smile sweet and still hand you the heavy end of the load.

And that's where I come in.

I grew up being the extra chair pulled to the table when somebody needed something and the first one folded up when the room got quiet. I was the family spare tire—only remembered when somebody was stranded. Five dollars' worth of help turned into four stops, two favors, and a stranger tagging along, all wrapped up in the bow of "But we family, right?"

So I learned early how to stop asking questions.

Not because I didn't notice, but because every answer came dressed in Sunday lies.

I watched grown folks—grandmamas with soft hands, uncles with loud laughs, and women who smiled like church fans in July—practice the fine Southern art of pretending. Pretending not to know. Pretending not to hear. Pretending the past wasn't buried just past the treeline.

Regret lives thick in places like that.

It seeps into the walls.

It rattles when people raise their voices too fast.

They said I was "too much," but what they meant was too awake. I noticed how blame rolled downhill and somehow always landed on me. How problems were passed around like plates at a potluck until my hands were the only ones left holding them. I learned the pattern so well I could hum it like a hymn.

And still—I stayed soft longer than I should have.

That's the Southern part of me.

The believing. The waiting. The hoping that folks would choose right if given one more chance.

But there comes a moment—quiet, holy, and final—when a woman realizes she is not a mule, not a shield, not a sacrifice. That moment met me like dawn after a long storm.

I didn't raise my voice.

I didn't swing back.

I simply stood up straight.

See, freedom doesn't always come loud. Sometimes it comes like a locked door you finally stop knocking on. Like setting down a weight you were never meant to carry. Like understanding that your truth doesn't need permission to breathe.

They can keep the mess.

They can keep the noise.

They can keep the pretending.

What I kept was my mind.

My voice.

My life.

And down here, that's how you really win.

Because in the South, a woman who frees herself—

is more dangerous than any lie ever told.

CHAPTER 60 — GOD SAT AT THE TABLE

Mama,

I'm writing you the way the South writes truth—slow, honest, and with God sitting right here at the table.

Some days I still don't understand why your time was so short. Twenty-eight years feels like a breath, not a lifetime. But God reminds me that "Precious in the sight of the Lord is the death of His saints" (Psalm 116:15), and that tells me Heaven didn't take you by accident. You were called, not cut off.

I carry your birthday with me, Mama. Not as a wound, but as a witness. February 28, 1978—life, not loss. When folks tried to mark me with it like a sentence, God whispered back, "Before I formed you in the womb, I knew you" (Jeremiah 1:5). And He knew you too. Every tear. Every prayer you didn't get to finish out loud.

I want you to know—I'm still standing.

It hasn't been easy being here, guiding my sister, holding together pieces that other folks dropped and walked away from. Family don't always look like family down here, and God knows that truth better than any of us. But His Word says, "When my father and my mother forsake me, then the Lord will take me up" (Psalm 27:10). And Mama, He has taken me up. Every single time.

There are nights I hear you in my own voice—soft, steady, and sure. I know that's no coincidence. God promised me, "I will not leave you comfortless" (John 14:18), and sometimes comfort sounds just like the woman who first taught me how to be brave.

To anyone reading this—understand this:

God sees what families hide.

He heals what silence tries to rot.

And He restores what love was supposed to protect.

Mama, rest easy.

Your story didn't end with you. God braided it into mine. And "All things work together for good to them that love God" (Romans 8:28)—even the parts that hurt, even the parts that don't make sense yet.

I'll keep walking.

I'll keep believing.

I'll keep telling the truth with grace.

Until the day God lets us sit and talk without time between us—

Know that I'm okay.

Sealed in faith,

held by God,

and forever your daughter.

Amen.

ENDING 61 — WHAT I KEPT

Down South, the road always looks longer before it opens up.

That's where my story settles—not in the dust, not in the noise, but at the place where God finally says, "Rest now. I've got you."

I came up learning how to endure more than I was meant to carry. Folks mistook my quiet for permission and my strength for availability. I was expected to hold what others dropped, to keep peace that wasn't planted in me, to survive storms I didn't summon. And for a long while, I did—because faith teaches you how to stand even when you're tired.

But God never confused endurance with destiny.

There was a season when everything felt heavy—memories looping like cicadas in July, family wounds that wouldn't heal right, grief that showed up uninvited. Still, the Lord kept me. He kept my mind clear and my heart tender. He taught me that not every door is meant to be reopened, and not every table deserves my presence.

In the South, we say, "Let it be," but God taught me the deeper meaning: let Him be God.

I learned that some people are lessons, not lifetimes. That love doesn't bruise. That peace isn't loud—it's steady. And that forgiveness doesn't mean returning to harm; it means releasing the weight so your hands are free for what's next.

When I finally stopped explaining myself, Heaven breathed easier around me. When I stopped fighting to be understood, God began doing the revealing. What was hidden came into the light—not with shame, but with clarity. Not to embarrass anyone, but to free me.

Now, the air feels different.

I wake up with gratitude instead of dread. I hear God in the small things—morning light through the window, quiet prayers answered without fanfare, a calm that doesn't depend on anyone else's behavior. The road didn't end; it widened.

This is the final destination:

not revenge,

not resentment,

but rest.

A place where I know who I am and whose I am.

A place where my story is no longer survival—it's stewardship.

A place where God's goodness isn't a promise I'm waiting on, but a reality I'm walking in.

Down South, we believe what's meant for you won't miss you.

And it didn't.

I arrived whole, held, and, finally, home.

 The end.

Faith-Based Conclusion — Held by His Hand

In the end, it was never about proving my strength—it was about trusting God with my softness.

Every mile I walked, He was already ahead of me. Every tear I cried, He counted. Every prayer I whispered when my voice shook, He heard. What I thought were delays were divine coverings. What I thought were losses were mercies in disguise. God was not absent in my waiting—He was intentional.

I learned that faith doesn't always move mountains; sometimes it teaches you how to rest at the foot of them and let God do the moving. I learned that obedience is louder than explanation, and peace is the truest confirmation. When I released what hurt me, God replaced it with what healed me.

The South taught me how to endure, but God taught me how to live.

I no longer question why things unfolded the way they did. I trust the Author. I trust the timing. I trust the hand that carried me when I couldn't carry myself. What was meant to break me refined me. What tried to silence me taught me how to listen to God instead.

This is my conclusion:

God is faithful.

Grace is sufficient.

And nothing surrendered to Him is ever wasted.

I close this chapter not empty but full.

Not weary, but wise.

Not afraid, but anchored.

Still believing.

Still becoming.

Still held.

Amen.

About the Author

Kalena Amos is a Southern woman shaped by faith, refined by fire, and held together by grace. Her story is not one of perfection but of perseverance—of learning how to trust God when answers were delayed and how to remain tender in a world that often demanded hardness.

Raised in the spaces where silence spoke loudly and strength was expected early, Kalena learned to lean on God not as a last resort but as a lifeline. Writing became her way of praying out loud—of releasing what was heavy and honoring what healed. Every page she writes carries the imprint of endurance, forgiveness, and hope rooted in Christ.

Kalena believes that faith is not about having it all together but about knowing who holds you together. She writes for women who have loved deeply, endured quietly, and trusted God even when the road felt long. Her words are meant to comfort, to tell the truth gently, and to remind the reader that softness is not weakness—it is strength under God's care.

When she is not writing, Kalena is choosing peace, guarding her heart, and continuing to walk in obedience, trusting that what God has for her will arrive right on time. Lil Southern Belle is not just her story—it is her testimony.

She writes with hope.

She lives by faith.

And she believes the best chapters are still being written.